THE ULTIMATE

facebook

LEAD

MACHINE

Real Strategies revealed that have produced, millions with
Facebook Ads

JAMES DICKS

Commerce Publishing

Lake Mary, Florida

THE ULTIMATE FACEBOOK LEAD MACHINE

ISBN 978-0692977255

This publication designed to provide accurate and authoritative information in regard to the subject matter covered. It is sold with the understanding that neither author nor the publisher is engaged in rendering legal, accounting, or other professional service. If legal advice or other expert assistance is required, the services of a confident professional person should be sought.

-From a declaration of Principles jointly adopted by a Committee of the American Bar Association and a Committee of Publishers.

For More Information, Please write:
103 Commerce St, Suite 140
Lake Mary, FL 32746
Or send email to: info@jamesdicks.com

Dedication

This book and project is dedicated to my family. It takes a tremendous amount of time to be an entrepreneur, and my family has always understood the sacrifice it takes, so my deepest thanks go to Deb, James and Jacki, as well as to my father James E. Dicks, Sr. He was a great mentor, entrepreneur and businessman who just passed away on September 12th, 2017 and will be much missed.

I also want to recognize the team it takes to create projects like this. Thanks to Ian for the long days, to Scott for your tremendous insight and over 25 years of friendship, to Tyler for always holding down the fort, to Dave for getting it done one way or another over 35 years of friendship, to Rocky for always believing and staying strong with the team for the last 10 years, and to Luis, our newest addition to the team who is already a huge contributor. I also want to make a special shout out to Jay and Julie, who have always worked tirelessly with me on book projects. You two are the best, and I enjoy working with you each and every time.

Special thanks also go to those serving their country in the armed forces, which less than one percent of Americans do. Of that number, more than half of them are in the Guard and Reserve, so they have a second job with employers who understand and support their commitment. Our freedom is not free, and it takes a tremendous sacrifice to serve — in some cases, even the ultimate sacrifice. Thank you to who now serve or have served.

THE ULTIMATE FACEBOOK LEAD MACHINE

Table of Contents

THE ULTIMATE FACEBOOK LEAD MACHINE

THE ULTIMATE FACEBOOK LEAD MACHINE

THE ULTIMATE FACEBOOK LEAD MACHINE

THE ULTIMATE FACEBOOK LEAD MACHINE

THE ULTIMATE FACEBOOK LEAD MACHINE

THE ULTIMATE FACEBOOK LEAD MACHINE

About the Author

How did I get to be one of the leaders in online digital social media marketing? Well, after years of financial regulatory expansion in the United States, my business was virtually forced out of my industry. I simply could no longer afford to do business in the United States any — not if I wanted to stay within the industry I had been in for the past 15 years anyway.

With respect to my business background and where I have been, I started marketing 30 years ago, and perhaps even 40+ years ago if you count the Gannett Rocks I used to sell to tourists at my father's Ski Resort when I was 6 years old. My entrepreneurial spirit has never since slowed down.

Amusingly, while I was selling the rocks on the tour buses by walking down the aisles, my year-younger sister thought holding out an ice bucket and putting on a smile was easier. Of course, everyone thought she was so cute that she made a lot more money than I did.

I first started working in the information education industry by utilizing direct mail as a primary method to attract potential customers, which then lead me to newsprint and direct print magazines. All of these are great vertical advertising mediums but scalability was always a limiting factor. By this I mean that there were only so many addresses you could buy in a specific area.

Those background experiences lead me to get into long form commercials. I have now personally worked in all facets of this business including as producer and executive producer of some of the most successful long form commercials ever seen in America.

I learned long ago that people buy from people, and I had my chance to be one of the people that people buy from early in my financial career. I created a User Interface that allowed a customer to access the world's financial markets. I built and outfitted a 24/7 data center that aggregated financial data straight from the exchange floors.

I took all of my institutional marketing experience and applied it to my new financial business. I also started using long form commercials, direct response, etc. to get customers to attend one of my live events. I found that the best thing about employing TV time as a marketing option is it is highly scalable. I have dedicated a complete chapter in this book on building a marketing plan to the point of diminishing returns.

I would now like to fast-forward to the last ten years and share how I ended up as a leading expert on Facebook marketing. During the Great Recession after the 2008 Financial Crisis, my financial business became strained to say the least, and the over-regulated landscape was just too much for me to manage anymore. My business went from a zero net capital requirement to a $50 million net capital requirement in a matter of a few years. I ultimately stopped doing business in the United States as a result. Yes, that was disappointing, and I as a former United States Marine am all about doing business and hiring in the United States, but the reality I was facing meant this was not entirely effective or practical.

I therefore decided to take my business offshore and start looking for customers using an international footprint. That was going to be a tough mountain to climb, as I had no international customers at that point. I have operated international businesses before, and in the past I had developed those sales channels from on-the-ground strategies where I would visit the country personally and develop a personal relationship with prospective new customers.

As anyone who has tried already knows, building a business face-to-face can be expensive in the modern era. Just think about how adding an ocean or two in-between your business and your prospective new customer, and the costs can climb quickly. In most cases, building an international business was just not feasible.

The problem for me and my business were that we had just come out from the end of a very tough financial situation, as were most business during the latter part of our Great Recession. I simply could not implement the same marketing strategies I had used in the past in my new business. In fact I am not even sure they would have worked, since the entire world's financial landscape had changed.

I needed a way to attract customers from around the world while maintaining a small footprint. I wanted to build a leaner and more profitable business this time around. To do that, I had to think outside the box, and Facebook allowed me to do just that.

I therefore turned to Facebook to help me build a new

international client base. Today I have tens of thousands of people that have registered for my services, and new clients are coming in the door each and every day. My business revenues are on the rise, and Facebook advertising is now my number one go-to marketing strategy.

I look forward to sharing with you how you can also use Facebook in your business. I will show you how to use Facebook to represent and promote your business online. I will tell you how to generate new business leads, find new customers, educate existing customers, and support those customers, all using Facebook. You will learn how to create creditably for both you and your business using Facebook. You will also learn how to create top producing ads that can build your business to a scale that you never imagined was possible.

Let me give you some perspective on my new beginning, since, like many business operators in the United States at that time, I was faced with tough economic realities. My business went from being a large thriving business to one that had suffered considerably during a widespread and deep recession. My business activities primarily focus on the United States. We used to do our business on a face-to-face level, something that I had learned to do while very young. Since I was taught that people buy from people, I developed a business centered on promoting myself as a personality that people would want learn from.

In this book, I will reveal the same strategies that helped me build a great business that thrived and had its start during those economic tough times. The first step I took was to look abroad, since I simply could not do business in the United States any longer. Quite frankly, this really was not such a bad thing. The growth rate for my overseas business was in the double digits versus the single digit growth rates I was able to achieve in the United States.

I also began using Facebook with a new sense of hope that it would help me grow my flailing business. As with most business that market online, we started spending some advertising dollars on Google. Using Google ads was not new to me, and I had used them in the past, but I was not overly-excited about using Google for marketing then, and I remain so now. Certainly you can get leads and customers from Google when people are searching for your keywords, etc. Unfortunately, in my industry, the keywords I wanted to use had gotten very expensive. When I first started using Google, my keywords were a nickel or ten cents, and I noticed that other businesses were even using my name as a keyword! Now, using the same keywords can be as high a $100 each. Such high keyword prices were just not efficient or cost-effective for me at that point.

I quickly realized that Facebook was going be a great opportunity for my business and family, as well as for my employees to see the opportunities of growth overseas. In just three short years, I was able to really dial into how I could use Facebook to create a real difference in my business. The first two and a half months were largely spent learning the ropes of Facebook marketing, but it was the last six months of that time when we really saw a big difference in our business growth. So don't worry, since what I am sharing with you will not take you three years. In fact you can use start using the strategies I present in this book to see a difference in a few short weeks to your business' bottom line.

I do not think Facebook's creators originally really understood just how big an economic impact adding its business solutions and advertising would have on their own bottom line. Certainly they are now leaders in the online digital media advertising space. Since well before Facebook went public, I have maintained that they would eventually create tremendous revenue for their shareholders. When all the stock analysts were saying the company was overvalued, I said to myself that there will be no company that will not be successful if it has access to information on over a billion people of reasonable means and that can track what those people are interested in, especially if they play their cards right.

Facebook currently has access to over 2.1 billion people, and they allow you to market to those people to offer your strategies, your business proposal, your products and your services. To take advantage of this huge global market, you just need to know how to use Facebook and how to implement its marketing abilities within your business, since that is exactly what I did. I really started to dive into Facebook and learn effective strategies on how to be able to use Facebook to grow our business internationally; using both paid advertising as well as organic advertising that results from people simply sharing what they are interested in with others.

Of course, one of the concerns I had during my learn curve was that I witnessed Facebook often changing their algorithms and had to adapt to this. The way Facebook delivers your message, the way they deliver your ads, and many other factors can influence your eventual success in using it as a marketing medium for your business.

I eventually concluded that it is now more expensive to advertise on Facebook than it was before, but just because you are not getting cheap $5 leads anymore, that does not mean you want to throw in the towel. For example, a client of mine is now getting leads for $17 versus costs of as much as $1,000 each prior to their use of Facebook.

As long as you are getting a quality Return on Investment or ROI from your Facebook advertising, then you should continue to spend until you reach the point of diminishing returns. In this case, my client was getting more than a 5 to 1 return on their investment, so my advice to them was to keep spending on Facebook ads!

Facebook is a business, and they certainly are doing something right considering their impressive revenue growth. Perhaps due to that fact, they often tweak their algorithms to make even more money. In the past, you could post or share a message on your Facebook timeline, and all those that were your friends or following your business page would be able to see your content.

Unfortunately, that is no longer the case, and your post's visibility on your followers' news feeds is now at an all-time low as I watched it go from 100% of your followers seeing your messages to less than 2%. It seems like the only way you can ensure that more of your followers see your message is to pay Facebook to boost your post. This lets you advertise your post to those that like or follow your business page. You can also create other audiences to see your message if you choose.

Personally, I have found it effective to boost my posts on a weekly basis. I first choose to boost posts to people that like my page, and then I boost a few posts a week to other people that I am targeting using Facebook's custom audiences feature.

I use Facebook for my business with the objective of getting both organic and paid advertising, so to do that I focus on tracking those metrics I get from my customers' journey. I also use landing pages to further promote my offers. I also use WordPress and Leadpages, depending on what sort of marketing I am doing.

Then I create tracking links to track where customers are coming from. For example, I determine if they are clicking on a signup link on my Facebook header, or if they going to my website and clicking a signup button there, or if they clicked on a post and signed up there. I also see how useful a paid post seems versus an organic post to my objectives. I track those by sending them to unique links so that I know exactly where the customer is coming from. I do that so that I can create custom messages that are better targeted to the experience of those customers I wish to attract.

I have also dedicated a chapter of this book to using Infusionsoft, which is what I use, and many of my clients now use. This software helps you automate the marketing and sales activities for your business, including email marketing, capturing leads and doing e-commerce.

Throughout this book, I will cover many things you can do on Facebook to generate leads. These include things like global pages, verified pages, boosting posts, creating marketing campaigns using the ads manager, and using the Power Editor Facebook provides. Still, all those tools really do not mean much unless you can utilize them in a concise marketing campaign that will allow you to strategically use those processes in your business on a daily basis to increase your company's revenues.

Largely thanks to Facebook, my business now has thousands of people coming in every day to use our products and services. During my testing phase, I spent hundreds of thousands of dollars and made many mistakes as part of my learning processes, but I have now built a tremendous business using Facebook.

As a result of my success and expertise, I've even had other businesses offer to pay me to do business on Facebook for them, as well as to create marketing strategies for them and help them close the loop between leads and sales. I have now put that information into this book, so that you too can employ the various different marketing strategies, options, products and services Facebook offers to build your own ultimate Facebook lead machine.

Foreword: Building a Bigger, Better Business with Facebook

I think we have all followed Facebook at some point, and many of us have used Facebook to connect to others for one reason or another. Facebook has gone thru many variations since the early days of its founding in 2004 on the steps of Harvard University.

If you are not using Facebook in your business today, then you are not maximizing the income potential of your business. This book will discuss how you can use Facebook to take your business to the next level and help you build the financially secure life you have always wanted.

I have spent years testing and developing strategies to help build my business and those of the many others who have reached out and hired me to do the same for them. After millions of dollars spent testing ad verticals, creating strategies and running ads, it is now time for me to share some of what I have learned over the years.

Remember, people are still joining Facebook in droves, and the more people that are using Facebook, the better for all of us that already use Facebook to help build our business.

I now challenge you to read carefully through this book and encourage you to look at it as more of a reference guide for promoting your business on Facebook than some book you just buy and leave on the shelf. I will share with you practical strategies that you can use in your business to grow your customer base. As with almost anything written today, you can probably find some of the same information online free, but nothing will replace having a mentor like myself, who has already successfully blazed the trail before you and who has spent their hard earned dollars testing and using the exact same marketing strategies they are now sharing with you.

I have gone through that learning process, and I have made many mistakes along the way as I learned to use Facebook in my business, using both paid and organic advertising strategies alike. The most important thing I can tell you is that if I am not the mentor for you, then please go out and find one that is right for you since your business probably cannot afford not to use what Facebook offers. One thing to know about mentors is that the information they pass on may well be the same information that is typically already out there, but they just deliver it in their own unique ways to those who wish to learn from them.

On caveat I want to mention, is that Facebook does have a rather annoying habit of making changes all the time, so I am often trying to hit a moving target by writing this book. For further updates on the information contained here and new ideas that occur to me, you can always start following me on Twitter @JamesEDicks or on Facebook at:

www.facebook.com/dnapulse

I know I have a lot to offer when it comes to marketing, since I have been doing it for over 30 years. One of the things I have always worked hard to do over the years was to memorialize my process and institutionalize my knowledge, and I have been able to do this across many vertical markets. I believe strongly in the power of new media like Facebook, but not necessarily as just one example of a vertical marketing option. In my opinion, it just happens that Facebook is the best thing around today when it comes to marketing.

I also believe that Facebook is still in the early stages of its life cycle, and we have yet to see how incredibly useful it will eventually turn out to be for businesses. I have followed the company for a long time, and I have invested in it ever since it became possible to do so. Everything I will share with you in this book is applicable to your business, and the marketing strategies I describe are the very ones that I feel will turn out to be most profitable for you.

Remember, Facebook means many things to many people, and it is interesting to hear some of the feedback from the various age-diverse groups out there. I am the state chairman for a volunteer organization, and when I first started to implement Facebook as one of our primary ways to communicate, I encountered some interesting feedback between these age groups.

The +70 group was mostly not interested in using Facebook, since they "never have and never will". I think that this reluctance has already started to change, and it will continue to do so as Facebook's age diversity increases with time from its inception in 2004. That being said, the +70 group was really in the realm of not understanding the social aspect of the Internet. In many cases, they seemed much more concerned about having their identity stolen than about enjoying the social aspects of communicating with others via Facebook.

As an interesting aside, I actually spent time with people from this age group working one-on-one to set them up with a Facebook page. I taught them how to post information on their timeline and how to connect with others. They got it, and it was truly amazing to see how fast they really embraced it when someone took the time to walk them through the process.

It is no secret that many people once thought of Facebook as a way to connect to all those old girlfriends and boyfriends they might have had. I might even be led to believe that Facebook could have been a leading cause of divorce at one time. Still, Facebook has morphed dramatically since then and its social influence has risen substantially, as is especially well-evidenced by its staggering growth in users and revenue.

I clearly recall Facebook announcing its advertising revenue in 2Q15 of $4.04 billion, which represented a huge increase of 39%. Monthly active Facebook users then numbered 1.31 billion people out of a total user based of 1.4 billion — which was up 13% from the same quarter of the previous year. Even then, that steeply growing number amounted to 20% of the entire world's population! According to analysts, Facebook's future growth will rely on marketing activities and increased user time spent on the platform. Furthermore, Facebook's acquisitions — including WhatsApp Messenger, Instagram, and Messenger — will ensure that inorganic growth continues for the long term on the platform.

What does that mean to us? Our business' will see higher revenues if we can embrace the technology and use it in our marketing plans. With any technology, the hard part is to actually apply it to your business and create the processes that will allow you to duplicate the success of it and translate that into increased revenue.

This book is specifically about using Facebook in your business, although I still use other mediums of marketing and support in my business. That being noted, the majority of the marketing I do is on Facebook. I am a firm believer of investing in marketing strategies until diminishing returns are seen. As long as my marketing strategies return positive results, I will spend to the point of diminishing returns. I will share more details about that later in this book.

Furthermore, it makes no sense to take something that works and only allow it limited success. Most businesses overlook this very simple strategy. Yes, a case for scalability exists and that goes hand in hand with spending until diminishing returns are seen, but Facebook has the scalability you need. I was concerned about that when I first started advertising on Facebook, and that was how I ended up building my marketing strategies using the diminishing point of return theory. I still have not yet gotten to that point in my business.

A case certainly exists for diversification, and we will discuss that later in this book as well, although I think the mere fact that most business fail to use a diminishing return on investment strategy means we should spend some time on how to implement marketing strategies that allow us to capitalize on the total market size available to us.

The pages in this book will follow my personal and business journey using Facebook. In addition to outlining the mechanics of advertising on Facebook, I will share some stories from other business that I have consulted with and that are now using some of the same strategies that I will share with you. I think the most exciting thing thru my journey of using Facebook in my business is the constant flow of requests I get to share my secrets with others.

Some business operators simply do not want to do it themselves, so they ask me and my team to do it for them. The number of requests I received grew so fast that I simply could not engage in them all, which was another valuable lesson I learn from this process. When you love doing something, be sure to always look for the opportunities to continue to do it. Basically, I built another business doing for others exactly what I am sharing here with you for a fraction of the price.

For more than seven years, I have dabbled in using Facebook for my business using the early advertising tools that were available on the platform, and I enjoyed the largely social aspect of sharing what I did with others. Still, it was the last three years that I really delved into how to maximize all Facebook has to offer and which has changed my financial future forever.

I will admit that Facebook is so expansive and offers so much that I simply do not know everything there is to know about it and probably never will. Facebook understands how important the functionally it offers is to businesses. Because of that, Facebook has already spent a lot of manpower and resources building the next generation of the business services we currently have available to us today. Their innovation will never stop, in my opinion.

While I might not know all of what Facebook has to offer, I can assure you that because of how much money I spent and continue to spend advertising on that platform each month, I have had the privilege of inside access to some of their programmers' and special business services that are reserved for only the largest advertisers. This access has allowed me to gain inside information that I know will help you and your business create a successful marketing campaign using Facebook.

Chapter 1: Introduction to Facebook

In the modern world teeming with social networks, Facebook has one of the fastest growth rates in the world. This chapter will introduce what Facebook offers and how that can help you grow your business.

Facebook Introduction

Facebook's website was specifically designed to allow users to register and create a free account and develop a Facebook profile in which they can include different information on themselves, their cause or their business.

In addition, a Facebook user can share a variety of media types with others, including pictures, music, video and text content. The image below shows what is now the very highly recognizable Facebook logo used on the company's website:

Figure #1: The Facebook Logo.

It can safely be stated that among users of social networks today, very few — if any — have not yet heard of Facebook, and many people have used Facebook for over

THE ULTIMATE FACEBOOK LEAD MACHINE

a decade since it started in 2004.

Some people in the business world may still find this online social networking platform rather new and unfamiliar, although the buzz about it may have generated an aura of excitement they sense could bring in extra profits. If they are not already actively using Facebook, many business owners probably feel they could really use a primer on some of Facebook's more effective marketing strategies.

This is precisely why this book was conceived. It will start by answering the question, "What is Facebook?" and will cover the platform's principal features and uses from a businessperson's perspective. The goal of doing this is to help a business produce significant amounts of valuable publicity and to create a powerful lead generator for a commercial enterprise.

Facebook's mode of operation is basically simple and easy to understand. The way the social networking part of the system works is that every Facebook account holder can connect voluntarily with other Facebook users of their choice to share their information and other content with.

The connection process begins with the user sending other Facebook users a "friend request". Upon accepting, the recipient of the request agrees to share their information with the sender of the friend request. This two-sided feature allows users to decide if they want to be connected to or avoid connecting to other Facebook users who approach them.

From the time of its founding roughly fifteen years ago,

Facebook has consistently improved its privacy protection and content management mechanisms for individuals sharing information. Currently, every Facebook user has the capability to cluster their connections into different groups and define which profile sections can be viewed by specific members or groups and which content can be shared publicly.

How Businesses Can Benefit From Facebook

A business with a Facebook page has the following advantages over its competitors who do not:

- **Accessibility:** Facebook gives the public access to the business. When a search for the business is conducted on Facebook, the business and its products or services can easily be found by potential clients.
- **Connectivity:** Once connected on Facebook, customers can easily engage in one-on-one conversations with the business page's administrators. They can also like the page, review the business, read other people's posts, and share its posts and photos with their friends after they visit the page.
- **Timeliness:** A Facebook business page can reach large groups of people in a timely manner with messages specific to their needs and interests.
- **Insight:** The analytic features of Facebook pages can give any business owner a deeper understanding of their customers and can serve as a basis for developing further marketing strategies.

THE ULTIMATE FACEBOOK LEAD MACHINE

Upon setting up a Facebook business page, the owner can request a custom Internet website address or URL, such as:

www.facebook.com/thecompanyname

This address can easily be placed on a business card and helps make their business even easier to locate online. To further advertise their Facebook business page, this simple address can also be included on the business' Internet website, brochures, newsletters, newspaper advertising, and in other printed marketing tools.

Keep in mind that a Facebook business page is a representation and extension of your business. The page provides an easy way for the business operators and their customers to share updates with large numbers of other people, which can be of the utmost importance in the modern information era. In addition, a Facebook page can readily promote a business and engage clients on both desktop and mobile platforms.

Besides the fact that a vast number of people can now be reached through Facebook, a business can also target a specific demographic of people who seem most likely to become its customers. This feature makes Facebook a great choice for a business currently operating without a website, as well as for one that already has an online presence.

If you are considering connecting with your business clients via Facebook, you may want to consider asking the following kinds of questions:

- What are the common elements shared by my business' ideal customers?
- What is the age group and location of customers and potential customers?
- What can my business offer them?
- Would any specific groups of people be more interested in:
    - a sale of certain products,
    - a timely offer of services, and/or
    - receiving messages from my business?

To broaden their business' online audience, an astute business owner can encourage customers and personal friends to like their Facebook page. These people are the most likely to see the business' posts on their Facebook News Feed.

In addition, Facebook offers a Build Audience feature, which allows the business owner to expand their Facebook audience for a nominal fee. The Build Audience feature lets you:

- **Invite Friends:** Let friends and family know about your business page. Their likes and support will increase the page's audience and help establish credibility by disseminating the information you provide on it in a timely manner.
- **Share the Page**: Make sure that you like your business page yourself. You are usually going to be one of the best spokespeople for your business and

probably already understand its strengths and weaknesses from a marketing perspective.

- **Invite Business Contacts:** Use your existing email contact list to notify people electronically about your new Facebook business page.

Bear in mind that having a Facebook business page is not necessarily all about the number of likes it receives, but more about genuinely connecting with people you contact through Facebook as potential clients and business leads.

Remember, when you really connect with people and they come to appreciate the product or service you are offering, they will take care of promoting your business and telling your story for you.

Facebook Page Types

Facebook offers three basic types of page to users that they can use to display information with. These include personal profiles, official and business pages, and groups. The following sections will describe each of these types in greater detail.

Personal Profiles

Originally, a Facebook profile was intended to represent a single individual and was not meant for commercial use. Such personal profiles would typically consist of photographs and the user's personal experiences that even might summarize their individual history from their own perspective.

Having a personal profile on Facebook also allowed an individual to personalize their page by uploading a profile picture, a cover photo and information such as their birthday, hometown, relationship status and work history. Personal profile owners can update their status, relate life events, and basically control the information published on their profile and timeline that they wish to share with other Facebook users.

In addition to editing their profile's content, the profile owner can add and message friends, use their News Feed to view friends' statuses, and share personal updates. Others with a Facebook profile can follow and see public updates from people that they are not friends with and can "like" pages to see updates on them in their News Feed.

Official and Business Pages

A Facebook Official or Business page is typically a timeline for an organization, cause, brand, business or public figure. Facebook business page owners can use this feature to their advantage to help generate leads for their enterprise. They can add a cover photo, provide directions, create mailing lists, post stories and host events, among numerous other capabilities. People that have "liked" their page can then see the page's updates displayed on their News Feeds.

While anyone can create a Facebook page, only the official representatives of an organization, business or public figure can create and manage a business or official page. To create a business page, a user must already have a Facebook profile from which they can manage multiple pages. Page creators can then give others permission to be administrators that can help with the management of the page.

If the goal of a Facebook page is promoting a specific company or raising brand awareness, then creating a unique page for the brand or business would probably be the best option. Through this page, the business owner can share special offers, promotions, make announcements and basically build a customer base and generate leads.

A Facebook business page can be created free of charge, and once set up, it can be optimized to have the same look across desktop and laptop computers, tablets, smartphones, iPods and other mobile devices. Facebook provides a Facebook Pages Manager app for Android and Apple's iOS that allows Facebook page owners to operate their page from anywhere and at any time they have access to the Internet.

Facebook pages come with several features not found on the profiles and group pages. The "Activity" tab on the page allows the user to manage messages, notifications and scheduled posts. In addition, an important section called "Insights" can help the page administrators track how posts are performing and who is connecting to the page. The Insight section breaks down the page's access by demographics and shares engagement information with its fan base, thereby helping the page owner gauge and understand who their company's fan base consists of. Page owners can change the visibility of its content in the "Settings" tab. The owner can choose who they want to post to the page, enable messages and set up profanity filters, among other features.

Much like profiles, Facebook page administrators can examine the activity log for published comments and posts. The log allows administrators to delete, hide or allow posts and comments.

Groups

As in some Internet discussion forums, Facebook group pages allow specific people with Facebook profiles, who have been added by the admins as members, to share data such as photos, updates and links among other members. A recent estimate of the number of people that use Facebook groups indicates that more than half a million people read and post to them each month, with thousands of new discussion groups created on a daily basis.

Group Facebook pages have many uses and are an excellent way for connecting peers, family, teammates, co-workers and others with shared interests. Members of groups can post about topics of common interest and related events. They can also follow conversations and comment on them, or even get information on job opportunities connected to the group. In addition, group pages allow the owner to send mass messages directly to the group members' inbox or News Feed.

Group pages offer three privacy settings. A summary of these options and their meaning is listed below:

- *Public Group*: Access is available to anyone who

wants to join or who has been added or invited by a member.

- *Closed Group*: Anyone can ask to join a closed group, but access is only available through an invitation or when added by a member of the group.
- *Secret Group*: Anyone can join the group, but they must be added or invited by a member of the group.

Differences between Business Use and Personal Use

Anyone interested in using Facebook for business purposes needs to understand the key distinction between a personal profile and a business page.

Not respecting this important difference could quickly get your business in trouble with the company's official policies, so the following sections will explain and contrast the established personal use of Facebook with its appropriate business uses.

What is a Facebook Profile?

A Facebook profile is simply a personal account of the user posted on Facebook.

When a user signs up for Facebook, they are immediately given a profile where they can add friends and family, upload photos, share videos and updates, and communicate on a personal level with friends.

Everyone that joins Facebook's social network gets a profile, with only one profile allowed to each person under their real name.

What is a Facebook Page?

A Facebook page typically represents an organization, cause, public figure or business. Facebook pages allow organizations and businesses to promote specials, provide information, and offer other perks to followers who have "liked" their page. In addition, having a page allows the business to use Facebook ads. Facebook places no limits on the number of pages you can manage under your profile.

Which should be used for Business: Facebook Page or Facebook Profile?

The question of whether to use a Facebook page or profile is easily answered in that using a Facebook profile for a business is a violation of Facebook's Terms of Service. A person should therefore use a profile, while a business should use a page.

Facebook can delete a profile if it is used for a commercial endeavor or does not use an individual's real name. Nevertheless, a Facebook profile is necessary to create a Facebook page. An existing profile can also be converted to a page.

What are the Advantages of a Facebook Page for Business?

Small businesses have much to gain from using a Facebook page to generate leads. Unlike profiles, where people must send a friend request before being allowed to make a connection, pages will connect with a person when they simply "like" the page.

People tend to hesitate when receiving a friend request when they don't know the person already. This simplified connection feature for pages allows potential customers and prospects to connect immediately with the commercial venture, thereby helping to create a substantial fan base for the business.

Another advantage of a Facebook page for business is the site's capability for tracking and measuring results. The "Insights" option allows the page owner to track the positive results and impact of their social media efforts. In addition, the page allows the user to take advantage of Facebook advertisements and launch contests on the page.

Basically, businesses can consider a Facebook page as a form of mini-website that can be used for commercial purposes, to generate business leads, to disseminate desirable information, and to directly engage customers and potential customers in a commercially relevant manner.

While there are numerous advantages to having a Facebook page for a small business these days, not having one can have some serious disadvantages. For example, the lack of a page could make people perceive that the business is antiquated and out of touch with social media users and technology in general. The lack of a Facebook page could also raise questions about the legitimacy of the business and about the level of progress the business is making. Having no Facebook page could also adversely affect the level of customer trust in the business.

Chapter 2: Setting Up a Business Page on Facebook

The time has finally come to start setting up your own business page on Facebook. The following sections will explain and walk you through this important process in detail.

Initial Setup

When setting up a Facebook page initially, you will need to enter the name of your page that you would like to have. Make sure that this page name is similar to your business name so that existing customers can easily find it, and also make it appealing to new potential clients.

You will then need to select from among the six main categories of page type. These page types each have subcategories specific to them that you will also need to choose from among. Keep in mind that it is important to make certain that you select the correct kind of Facebook page for your business.

To optimize the impact of your Facebook page, you will probably need to take some time to choose the best category and subcategory selections for your business. When making this selection, try to choose the types that are most likely to catch your desired audience's attention and that seem most applicable both to the content of your page and to your business purpose.

Fortunately, Facebook allows you to adjust the category of your page any number of times. This allows you considerable flexibility if you think you made an initial mistake when choosing a category or subcategory for your business. Keep in mind that changing a business category may result in an unintended loss of reviews or check ins for your business, and it might also cause the map directing clients to your business to be re-generated.

After taking that consideration into account, if you still want to change your page's category after initially selecting one, you can follow this procedure:

(1) Click the "About" button situated on the left side of your Facebook page.

(2) Click on "Page Info".

(3) Hover your mouse over the section entitled "Category", and click on "Edit".

(4) Choose another appropriate category from the menu that drops down initially, and then choose a suitable subcategory from the second menu that drops down.

(5) Click on "Save Changes".

Local Business or Place

When choosing an initial category for your business, you will probably want to select the category for "Local Business or Place". This is especially appropriate if your business has a physical address where your clients visit to transact business with you. This category is also appropriate for businesses that have a specific physical region in which its services are provided to customers.

Furthermore, choosing the "Local Business or Place" category allows potential or existing customers to check in with your business at its location and permits them to submit a review of your business via Facebook that are posted publically for others to look over.

One thing to keep in mind when choosing this category initially is that if you ever decide to change your business' category from the "Local Business or Place" category, your Facebook business page will lose any reviews or check ins that it initially had from your customers. Of course, this might be a good thing if you had initially received some negative reviews and wish to start again.

In addition, changing away from those categories may mean the map to your business generated by Facebook may change. This should not present much of an issue as long as the new map still provides potential clients with an effective way of finding your place of business if you will do business with them on site.

Company, Organization or Institution

You will probably want to select the category for a "Company, Organization or Institution" if your Facebook page pertains to an organization that has no specific location for its operations.

If you would like to provide a business address and allow customers to do check ins — but not to leave reviews — then this more general business category could be suitable even for a business that operates locally.

An example of the suitable use of this category might be for a Facebook page set up to promote a non-profit organization that provides food to under privileged school children free of charge. The page might feature communications from the organization's leaders, as well as showing photographic examples of the children being fed and providing information on how to get involved and donate funds to the group. Such pages will also usually have links to the organization's official website.

Brand or Product

If your Facebook page will be used to promote something that a variety of retail outlets may offer at more than one physical location, then you can select the "Brand or Product" category. This option is especially popular with those who prefer not to enter a specific physical address for their Facebook page.

A suitable example for using this type of category might be when a business offers a popular product like a food processor for sale through many retail outlets. They can dedicate a Facebook page to promoting this food preparation product to the public and could possibly use the page to suggest recipes that can be made using it.

Artist, Band or Public Figure

If your Facebook page will be used to promote a specific individual public person, then it may be appropriate for you to select the "Artist, Band or Public Figure" category. This tends to be an especially popular choice among those people who wish to market themselves separately from their personal Facebook profile.

An appropriate example for this category might include a politician who wants to endorse and disseminate their specific political views. In addition, a celebrity using either a real or fictional name might find such a category designation useful to market themselves to potential employers and to share their experiences with and promote their opinions to fans.

Entertainment

If your Facebook page does not mainly pertain to a specific individual but is instead primarily concerned with entertainment media like films, books, music, magazines, sports and games, you can select the Entertainment category. This category can also be a good option if you prefer not to provide a specific physical address with your Facebook page.

For example, a media production company might set up a Facebook page in the Entertainment category for a film it has just released and wants to promote via Facebook. The promotional page can include links to the film's trailers on YouTube, awards it has received, and positive reviews from film critics.

Cause or Community

When the activist effort or community organization you wish to create a Facebook business page for does not have a specific location, and hence fails to fall accurately under any of the primary categories mentioned above, you can instead choose "Cause or Community" as the main category for its Facebook page.

Before you choose this category, you will first want to make sure that you have reviewed the other choices carefully to ensure that your business' Facebook page is not better suited to be listed within a different category.

An example of the appropriate use of this category might be for an activist group that wishes to promote the cause of reducing the proliferation of cell phone towers in residential areas because they are concerned that such towers might expose the local community to potentially harmful radiation.

Example of Multiple Page Category Choices - Microsoft

If you find the selection of Facebook page categories somewhat confusing, you can consider the example of how a very well-recognized name like Microsoft Corporation has organized their business pages on Facebook.

First of all, Microsoft has its primary Facebook page entered under the category suitable for a "Company, Organization or Institution". Each of their individual Microsoft store locations then have separate Facebook pages that are placed under the "Local Business or Place" category. In addition, they also have Facebook pages dedicated to promoting specific branded items they sell, and which are listed in the category suitable for a "Brand or Product".

Choosing Page Administrators

Choosing a responsible and qualified administrator can be vital to the success and integrity of your Facebook page, and that key decision should therefore not be made lightly since the administrator will control the page's future and hence can have a major impact on your business' public image.

The original creator of the Facebook page is automatically assigned to be the page's administrator or admin. The primary administrator of a Facebook page is the only one who can alter the page's appearance and publish posts from the perspective of the page. In addition, only the administrator can assign roles to other people and change their existing roles.

Facebook page administrators are given general authority to make all changes for a page, and they can also authorize others to allow them to make specific types of changes to a Facebook page depending on their particular role. Including the page administrator, there exist five different role types for those individuals who the page administrator wishes to make responsible for managing a Facebook page.

In order to give someone a role to perform on a Facebook page you are interested in, you will either need to be its administrator or to ask its existing administrator to perform the role change.

If you are an administrator, you can follow the subsequent procedure to allow someone else to make changes to the

Facebook page you are managing:

(1) Click on the "Settings" text shown at the upper right of your Facebook page.

(2) Click on "Page Roles" situated in the column to the left.

(3) Type the person's name or email address in the resulting entry form. If the person you want to assign a role to is already your friend on Facebook, then you can start typing their formal name and choose it from the list that pops up. If they are not already your friend on Facebook, then you can type in their email address that they have associated with their Facebook account to find them.

(4) Click on the appropriate role you wish to choose for them from the menu that drops down. See the table below for a description of the abilities of each possible role.

(5) Click on "Save".

(6) You will then need to enter your Facebook password to confirm the change.

You can use this "Page Roles" menu to assign a new page role or to edit an existing page role and change a particular individual's management permissions for your Facebook page.

Depending on how the person you are changing the roles of has their Facebook settings configured, they might get an email or a Facebook notification of the change you made to their role for the page.

The table shown below in Table 1 shows each of the five page administration roles across the top, which are Admin, Editor, Moderator, Advertiser and Analyst. In addition, the table displays a "Yes" for each of the roles if a person in that role can perform the functions listed in the first column of the table or a "No" if they cannot.

Table #1: A list of Facebook page administrative functions and which administrative roles are able to perform them appears on the following page.

THE ULTIMATE FACEBOOK LEAD MACHINE

Functions They Can Perform	Admin	Editor	Moderator	Advertiser	Analyst
Manage page's roles and its settings	Yes	No	No	No	No
Edit the page and include new apps	Yes	Yes	No	No	No
Remove posts and add them as the page	Yes	Yes	No	No	No
Send a message as the page	Yes	Yes	Yes	No	No
Respond to posts and delete comments	Yes	Yes	Yes	No	No
Remove and ban people from posting	Yes	Yes	Yes	No	No
Create page ads	Yes	Yes	Yes	Yes	No
Review page insights	Yes	Yes	Yes	Yes	Yes
See who posted as the page	Yes	Yes	Yes	Yes	Yes

Edit Page Options

In order to change the various options associated with a Facebook page, you will first need to be an administrator. You can then access the page's Admin panel that is situated in the upper region of the page. You can also use this panel to review the progress of your page in terms of its success in publicizing your business, product or cause.

Within the Admin panel also lies the very important ability to set up your Facebook page and change its numerous options. For example, you can choose a profile picture for your Facebook page, you can select a suitable cover image for it, and you can edit the information listed about your page. In addition, you can post a status for the page, add media like images or videos, create events, add milestones and ask questions.

Profile Picture

The profile image used on your Facebook page can have a substantial impact on its promotion since this picture is the first thing people will see when they are searching for new pages related to your business. It therefore makes sense to create an impressive profile image, and having an attractive business logo that fits well within a square can suit this purpose admirably.

When creating this important profile picture for your page, remember to keep in mind that it can currently be uploaded as a 180x180 square image but it will only be displayed using a resolution of 160×160 pixels. Also note that Facebook automatically creates a reduced size image of only 50×50 pixel resolution from your profile picture that gets shown in Facebook search results, as well as along with any posts or page updates that may be seen by viewers or followers of your page.

Cover Photo

The cover photo of your Facebook page acts as the page's header and is another important way you can impact your audience. Not only does will this image be the largest image on your Facebook page and be situated right at the top, but a miniature image of your cover photo will be shown whenever a person links to your Facebook page in a Facebook post.

The exact dimensions of the cover photo allowed by Facebook sometimes change, but they are currently by pixels .

Since it can change with new updates, a Facebook page at the following URL exists to show you the current dimensions of both the cover photo and the profile picture as currently used by Facebook:

https://www.facebook.com/CoverPhotoSize/

Editing Your Settings

Once you have created an appropriate Facebook page for your business and uploaded the two primary images used to identify it, you will probably then wish to review and edit some of your page's settings as you deem necessary. You will need to have admin status in order to view and edit the settings for your Facebook page.

To find out your page's current settings and make changes to them, click in the top right corner of your screen on the word "Settings". From there, you will be sent to a page where you can select the type of settings you wish to update from the sidebar on the left side of the page.

This sidebar can change with future updates and varies somewhat with the type of page you have chosen, but it currently contains the following groups of settings:

- *General*: This settings group allows you to edit the basic settings for your page, such as: visibility, who can post to it and tag photos, whether reviews are permitted, whether any countries or ages are restricted from viewing it, if words or profanity should be blocked from the page and comment rankings. In addition, you can download the page, merge duplicate pages with it, and delete your page.
- *Messaging*: This settings group allows you to select how people can message your page, and it allows you to choose whether the Enter or Return key will send a message. You can also use the Response Assistant to set up instant messages and can review what your response time has been recently.
- *Edit Page*: This group of settings includes the ability to configure actions, as well as the various tabs that are displayed along the top of your Facebook page. You can also obtain the exact URLs for each tab on

your Facebook page so that you can link to it.

- *Post Attribution*: You can select whether your posts, likes and comments appearing on the page are initially attributed to your Facebook page or to your personal Facebook account. You still have the option to change the attribution for each post as you create or edit it.
- *Notifications*: Choose how and if you wish to be notified each time a Facebook event relative to your page occurs.
- *Page Roles*: Use this setting group to create new administrative roles for your page or edit them and assign people to fill those roles.
- *People and Other Pages*: This group lists the people who like your page and allows you to remove, ban or assign them administrative roles.
- *Preferred Page Audience*: Use this settings group to select and update the information about what sort of residential location, interests and age group you want Facebook to help put your page in front of.
- *Apps*: This settings group allows you to delete existing apps and suggests new apps you can add to your Facebook page that it may benefit from.
- *Instagram Ads*: You can connect and use a single Instagram account to run ads for your business.
- *Featured*: This settings group lets you add and delete your featured likes that you make as your page. It also allows you to add featured page owners whose personal information will be shown publicly in the page's About section and the page will be displayed on their personal profile.
- *Crossposting*: Use this settings group to share

videos among multiple Facebook pages that that have added each other.

- *Page Support Inbox*: This feature allows you to check up on support requests you made for your page.

Given the large number of settings that are available to you, it would make sense to click on each menu to get a better feel for what sort of settings you can select and how they might impact your Facebook page and hence the business you can hope to generate from it.

When setting up your page, note that a column of tabs is displayed in a vertical frame immediately under your Facebook page's profile image. Depending on what tabs you choose, it might look something like this:

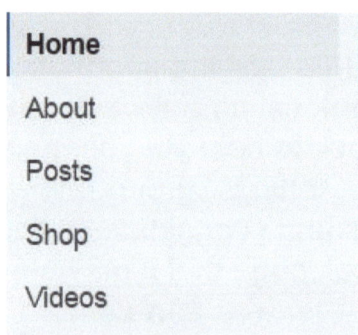

Home

About

Posts

Shop

Videos

A very important thing to keep in mind is that this column of tabs will only allow you to display roughly five tab entries at a zoom level of 100 percent before a viewer of your page may need to scroll down to see more.

As a result, those extra tabs beyond five effectively become invisible to many viewers, so make sure to adjust

THE ULTIMATE FACEBOOK LEAD MACHINE

your settings so that your page's most important and engaging tabs — including those that link to any key apps you plan on using — are among the initial five most visible ones.

You can edit the tabs that display in that list by clicking on the "Settings" text located at the upper right of your page and then clicking on "Edit Page" to the left. That will open up a list of tabs that you can reorder by picking them up and placing them where you want them to appear in the list by using your mouse to click on the icon to the right of each tab's name and then dragging it wherever desired.

You can also create new tabs from that menu by clicking on the button at the bottom of the tab list and entering its name. In addition, you can view and copy the URL for each tab by clicking on the Settings button next to it and then clicking on the Copy URL button that appears.

Managing Permissions

Most of your Facebook page's permissions can be managed using its Settings menu as described in the preceding section, which is easily accessed by clicking on the "Setting" text in the upper right corner of the page.

If you have initially used Facebook's default settings, you will especially want to review the General group of settings to make sure that the default permissions Facebook has chosen conform to those you want set up for your business page. In particular, you will want to make sure that your page's Page Visibility, Country and Age Restrictions, Visitor Posts and Tagging Ability have been reviewed and are deemed suitable for your business purposes.

In addition, if you want any other people to help you manage your Facebook page, you will want to update the Page Roles settings group to add their names and select their desired administrative roles. You can use the same group to edit admin settings for any people you need to change those settings for.

When it comes to deleting your page, you can do that under the General settings group. Using the Remove Page function will erase your page, photos and posts permanently. Since this cannot be undone, you will want to make sure that you back up all of the information you wish to keep before choosing to remove your page from Facebook.

Removing a page that has had a personalized URL set for it typically means that URL will be unavailable for at least two weeks after being deleted. If the URL remains unavailable after that time frame, an infringement form can be filed with Facebook asking to use the URL again. Rather than removing the page, you might find it easier to just hide it using the Page Visibility option under the General group of settings and selecting Unpublish Page.

Finally, if your Facebook page is promoting a business involving the consumption of alcohol, Facebook has an Alcohol-Related age restriction that sets the minimum age to view your page based on the viewer's location. This typically means that viewers who are less than 21 years of age cannot see your page, although you remain the one responsible for those who see your page on Facebook.

Verifying Your Page

Verifying your business Facebook page is an important and relatively easy step to take. Doing so tells your prospective customers that you are a legitimate business concern, you have an active Facebook page, and that you are taking your presence on Facebook seriously.

If your page's category is Company, Organization or Local Business, then you might be able to obtain a gray verification badge. Alternatively, if your page is for a celebrity, public figure, media, sports team, or entertainment, then you could qualify for a blue verification badge. These badges appear as a checkmark within a circle and are placed next to the page's name and in a search.

In either case, you will need to provide Facebook with proof of your concern's authenticity and meet the company's requirements for verification. The first step to take is to make sure that your Facebook page has a profile picture and cover photo set up and that you are an admin of it. The option to verify should then appear after you click on Settings at the top of your Facebook page and scroll down to Page Verification, click on Edit and then on Verify this Page.

You can either verify your page by providing a business phone number to which a verification code is sent that you will need to provide, or you can upload an image or electronic document of an official business document that displays the name of your business and its address.

If you prefer to use a business document, any of the following types will typically suffice:

- A business utility bill
- A business license
- A business tax file
- The certificate of formation for your business
- The articles of incorporation of your business

The business document you wish to use for page verification can be uploaded in many common document or image formats, including: .doc, .docx, .pdf, .jpg, .jpeg and .png formats.

Adding Apps

Applications, or apps as they are typically known, can be added to your Facebook page. Depending on what apps you select, they can help your page visitors get even more from your page than what basic use will allow, and they can also help you collect information from current or potential clients.

Apps can help you make you make better use of your Facebook promotions and can also help satisfy the particular needs of your viewing clients before they have even considered what exactly they are looking for from your business.

Of course, Facebook also offers a standard set of functionality for the business pages it hosts, and it is usually well worth reviewing the details of what they make available to you that might apply to your particular business.

Furthermore, many businesses use apps to include additional functionality on their Facebook pages, such as providing extra information about promotions and route maps to their location. They might also use apps to offer existing or potential clients access to the business offerings situated at other social media outlets, like Twitter for example.

If you are using Facebook Business Manager for your page, you will first need to click on "Use Facebook as my page" to obtain access to a search box that lets you find new apps to install. You should also remember to put any important app tabs in a prominent place among the top five tabs visible to the visitor.

When it comes to adding apps to your Facebook page, perhaps the easiest way to do so is to search Facebook for the names of ready-made apps created by other people that can be added to your page. Once you find the Facebook page for such an app, you need to go to that page and follow this procedure to add the app to your page:

(1) Click on the cover photo of the app page or click on the "Use App" button below the cover photo, if available.

(2) Click on the big "Add <app name> to a Page" button. If this button does not appear, the app cannot be

added to one of your pages.

(3) Use the dropdown menu to choose which of your Facebook pages you want to add the app to.

(4) Click the "Add Page Tab" button.

Those who want to write their own custom HTML apps will first need to add the Static HTML app to their Facebook page. You can search for "Static HTML" in the Facebook search bar to find the app's Facebook page, and then proceed as described above to add that app to your page.

Once you have clicked on the "Add Page Tab", you will get another screen with a "Set Up Tab". This will let you adjust settings for the page tab you have just installed.

In the Static HTML tab, you will then be able to enter the HTML code and any associated text that you wish to display on your Facebook page. For example, you can use this feature if you want to include a contact or sign up form on your Facebook page or if you would like clients to be able to post testimonials to your page.

You can also use the "Add a Button" button just below your page's cover photo to add an action button to your Facebook page that either runs an app or directs viewers to a website.

How to Remove an App from a Facebook Page

Sometimes an app or HTML tab you have added to your Facebook page will have served its purpose and therefore needs to be removed from your Facebook page. This can be achieved rather quickly by:

(1) Clicking on the "Settings" text located at the top right of your Facebook page.

(2) Then clicking on "Apps" in the menu appearing to the left.

(3) Then hover your mouse over the app you wish to remove and click the "x" on it.

Remember that performing this procedure will only remove the app from the page you are presently managing, and that if you manage multiple pages, you will need to remove it from all of them, if that is required.

How to Add Ready Made Applications

As mentioned briefly above, Facebook offers numerous useful applications that are already preinstalled on the platform and can be quickly installed on your page. For example, applications exist for running contests, purchasing tickets, collecting email addresses for mailing lists, and for operating complex e-commerce shops.

Most of these apps can be freely obtained from their Facebook pages, but some premium services may involve paying an extra to the application owner when they are added to your page.

To add Facebook Apps that are already posted on Facebook's network to a business page, you will first need to switch from your Personal profile to viewing your business' Facebook page. You can then search for the application you wish to install by typing its name within the Facebook search bar on the top menu.

For example, if you search for the popular app "Pagemodo", you will get numerous results, not all of which are apps. Scroll down to the one that says "App. 500,000+ Monthly Users" underneath the title and select that one.

Once you select that option, you will be directed to a page that allows you to install a custom tab or one of the company's free or premium Facebook apps by clicking a button. One of Pagemodo's most popular free apps allows you to obtain email addresses from people who want to sign up for a newsletter.

Once you select the app you want, the next page will ask you to specify the Facebook page you want to install it on. You will then be forwarded to that page and may be prompted to change the app's settings according to your preferences.

Mobile Access

Providing potential customers with information about your business on mobile devices so that they can contact and find it when they are away from home has clear advantages for many businesses. Fortunately, your customers can easily use Facebook on mobile devices in a variety of ways.

Access to Facebook is readily available via any Internet

browser installed on a mobile device. In addition, you can download the appropriate Facebook app for either the Android operating system that runs on many smart phones or for Apple's iOS that runs on iPhones and iPod Touches.

Login Approvals

One key thing for mobile users to keep in mind is that using Facebook on a mobile device may activate some of its security features, so it can help to get familiar with those in advance of going mobile.

Obtaining access to Facebook using a mobile device can be filtered via the system's security protocol known as "Login Approval". In this case, you will be asked to provide a security code if you log in to your Facebook account using a device Facebook does not recognize.

The security code will be sent to the telephone number that is connected to your Facebook account via an SMS message. If you have Login Approvals turned on, you can save it to your mobile device after entering your security code. This allows you to prevent having to do this every time you log in to Facebook. Also, Facebook's mobile app features the Code Generator function, which will generate a new security code for your account every thirty seconds.

You can adjust the Login Approval settings for your Facebook account from your Security Settings menu. These settings can be accessed by going to your personal Facebook page and clicking on the small triangle in the upper right hand corner of the page. You then need to select "Settings" from the resulting dropdown menu, and then choose "Security" from the menu to the left and click on the "Edit" text next to the Security Setting that says "Login Approvals".

The Facebook App

The Facebook app that has been developed to run on either the Android or iOS mobile operating systems is a special version of Facebook that has been optimized for usage on mobile devices.

Once the Facebook app has been downloaded to your mobile device, you can then use Facebook independently without having to open an Internet browser and log into Facebook.

The Facebook app even features a special mobile layout more suitable for smaller screens, and you can run the app in the background on your device to receive notifications.

Running the Facebook app in the background on your mobile device will keep you logged in even when the app is not specifically being used. This will permit you to continue to receive messages from friends and notifications via your mobile device almost as soon as they are sent.

Using Facebook with a Mobile Browser

Those who wish to obtain access to Facebook's features via an Internet Browser can also use their mobile devices for this purpose if a browser is installed and Internet access is available.

Facebook's website features a special layout for mobile devices that has been designed to facilitate navigation on smaller screens. This special layout has a similar appearance to the mobile app's interface.

If a user wants to turn this special mobile layout off, then they can choose the "Desktop Site" view from the menu. This will force the mobile device to display the Facebook website as if a desktop computer was being used to view it.

Syncing Your Contacts

The Facebook mobile app can be set up to sync your Facebook business contacts and friends with your mobile phone contacts. This process also adds your contacts' Facebook profile information to your phone contact records.

After syncing Facebook and your mobile phone, your Facebook friends will now appear in your list of telephone contacts along with the profile picture from their Facebook account.

This helpful function allows the active business person to further integrate their Facebook business page and contact list with the use of their mobile device.

The Voice Bar

An important feature of any Facebook business page is the so-called Voice Bar that appears directly below the page's cover photo. This indicator shows page administrators clearly whether they are currently posting, liking and commenting on behalf of the page or as themselves using their personal Facebook profile.

The benefit of having this bar is to help Facebook page admins avoid any confusion over their posting identity and possibly posting in an unintended voice.

The Voice Bar appears on the page as a light blue bar stretched over the top. It has an option for an admin to easily toggle between posting for the page and for their personal profile. The feature will help page owners avoid mistakenly posting or taking other actions using the wrong voice from what they had expected to use.

Why This Is Important for Marketers

A business oriented Facebook Page will often have admins from the company that do not actually manage the page but are instead admins because of their unique qualifications. For example, they might have the information required to update a certain tab; they might need to post a daily offer; or they may need to access the page's Insights for some reason.

Sadly, such people often lack substantial expertise in Facebook marketing, and they can seem oblivious to some of the finer points of operating a Facebook business page that are well understood by experienced marketers. They may not even be aware that when they liked or commented on the Facebook business page, that they had been doing so on behalf of the page using the business's brand instead of doing so as a personal user.

Most Facebook marketers would tend to agree that it is less than optimal to have admins liking something on their own page's news feed on behalf of the page itself, especially when they had intended to do so personally.

Potentially embarrassing marketing errors like this can give the business' management justifiable cause for concern from a marketing perspective when contemplating promoting relatively inexperienced assistants to serve as admins on a Facebook business page.

Fortunately, the availability of the Voice Bar now gives management a clear way to instruct new admins on how to avoid this potential marketing error by making sure they chose their personal profile for their "voice" on the page as soon as they get promoted to admins.

Why Marketers Also Need to Be Extremely Careful

Most marketers would agree that it seems better and more straightforward to address your audience on Facebook as yourself personally. This means you really need to be aware of the voice you are using when engaging with others on Facebook if you sometimes need to post on behalf of the brand you are promoting on the Facebook business page.

The Voice Bar feature is an especially useful tool because it allows admins to readily switch between using their brand to post, comment or like and using their personal profile instead. This feature also allows Facebook admins to avoid the potentially embarrassing situation where they might feel personally moved to defend the company against a negative comment someone left, only to later find out that they had inadvertently left the defensive comment under their company's brand rather than their personal profile.

Of course, being able to quickly change voices using the Voice Bar should also give careful marketers an efficient way to respond rapidly to another person's comment to support the company or cause they work for. Doing so lets them either perform quick damage control in case of a negative comment or to contribute to the enthusiasm about their brand if the comment were instead positive.

Basically, admins really need to be aware of what voice they are using on Facebook. Furthermore, it generally appears best for their company and viewpoint if they remain polite and respectful of all parties they engage with since that sort of behavior will also reflect positively on their brand.

Chapter 3: Facebook Content

We are now ready to talk about the content for your Facebook business page. You can utilize much of your existing written content and images, so now is a good time to start organizing that and breaking it up to share on Facebook in manageable portions.

Remember, Facebook generally shares less than 1% of your content to those that like your page since it wants you to pay to boost your content. Facebook also enables you to choose followers or to create a new custom audience to deliver your content to.

When it comes to marketing, I am also a big fan of testing as many variables in a controlled environment as I can. Once I do that, it's all about scalability. As an example, one of my clients was spending the majority of their budget on traditional media outlets that primarily consisted of print media, magazines, etc. We started them out on Facebook, and they immediately started to generate leads for their business. The client initially was seeing an average cost of $1,000 per lead generated, with a 3.2:1 return on investment. Now they have shifted almost their entire marketing budget to Facebook and are running at a cost of about $16-$18 per lead acquisition with a 6.2:1 return on investment. It is not hard to see where the company should continue to focus its marketing efforts.

The real question for them is whether they see an increase in sales conversion and value. Once again, I am a huge proponent of spending your marketing dollars to the point where you see diminishing returns. Only a few reasons exist to test and spend marketing dollars across other mediums if you have not spent them to a diminishing point of return on the current channels that are already producing a great return for you. One of those reasons is that you want a better sales conversion number and not just an improved lead generation result.

Let us focus on lead generation and conversion first, because if you fail to get the leads, then you have no one to sell to anyway. A successful business lead that ultimately results in a sale is known as a lead conversion, and it has a cost associated with it that depends on how you are marketing. In the above example, the company went from $1,000 per lead conversion using their former marketing methods to $20 per conversion using Facebook, and they were delighted with that result. Who wouldn't be, so why go anywhere else? I suggest you get as many of those cheap $20 lead conversions as you can while you are still able to. Just continue to spend on advertising until you see the cost per conversion number become unacceptable, and then pull back and look at using other media channels again.

Remember, if you want to sell on Facebook, then the best way to do that is by delivering a solution to a known problem that your existing client or ideal customer is having. Help educate them on how to solve it and then train and support them in implementing that solution. This type of engagement with your clients will not only foster a sale, but it will also help maintain their loyalty. The true measure of a successful business is the success of its customers. It is the longevity of your relationship with a customer that will create and extend the customer lifetime value that most businesses greatly benefit from.

The following sections will describe how to create, share and link content from elsewhere to the timeline of your Facebook business page, as well as how to add images and videos to your Facebook posts.

Written Content

Posting written content to Facebook will probably be a key form of communication via this medium with your existing clients and with potential customers for your business. Make sure this written content is of a consistently high quality, since having your thoughts well organized and using good grammar, spelling and punctuation in your text tends to reflect well on your business. Also, remember to keep your written Facebook posts as positive as possible when it comes to presenting your products and services.

To place written content on your Facebook page's timeline, you just need to navigate to your business' home page and start typing in the blank at the top of the timeline where it says "What's on your mind?"

You can also paste text into that same blank that you have previously prepared in a word processing program like Microsoft Word, for example. Using such a program first can be a very good idea, since such software usually checks text for spelling and punctuation errors, and doing this will allow you to catch those mistakes before posting text containing them to Facebook.

Shared Content

One of the most interesting and useful features of Facebook is the ability to share content posted elsewhere on Facebook on your own timeline, as well as with your followers and friends.

Also, sharing Facebook content sends an alert to the person who originally posted it that you are doing so, which can help bring in new views and potential followers to your Facebook page and ultimately more clients for your business.

Linked Content

Not all of the content posted on your business' Facebook timeline needs to be of your own creation. Many page admins also like to post links to relevant articles or positive reviews about the company's products that are posted elsewhere online.

Another way to use links to your business' advantage is to employ the Facebook page linking strategy, which you should use whenever applicable since it helps generate exposure for your page. Basically, when you are posting written content to Facebook and you happen to like another relevant Facebook page, you can link to that page in your written posts.

For example, DNAPulse likes the company Harley Davidson, which is one of my clients. So, when I post on DNAPulse's Facebook page and want to mention Harley Davidson, I would simply type in the "@" sign (i.e.

@harleydavidson). When I do that, I get a pop up menu of Facebook pages that I can choose among to link to. Including Facebook page links in this manner will help improve the organic deliverability of your content, and it may also get the attention of clients whose pages you link to since they will receive a notification about it from Facebook.

You may also want to use a "#" or hashtag in your written Facebook posts. I advise using only one of these per post, since there is no need to use more, and using the "#" is really more of a Twitter thing anyway. Facebook users do employ them, but you'll be penalized for using too many.

Photo Content

The next important addition to your business Facebook page's content will be images. These can include photographs, cartoon graphics, artwork and logos. A particularly popular type of image-containing content posted to Facebook involves first taking a background image and then putting relevant text over the image to make a point.

You can upload an image to your Facebook business page by navigating to its home page and looking at the top of its timeline just above the blank containing the phrase "What's on your mind?" There, you will see a button to upload a Photo or Video. Click on that button, and a window will open up that allows you to either upload a photo or video, or create a photo/video album. Select Upload Photo/Video and then use the resulting window to browse on your computer to the location of the image you wish to post.

Select that image, and click on Open.

Facebook accepts images saved in the .png and .jpg or .jpeg image file formats. The standard resolution for images displayed on Facebook seems to be 180 by 180 pixels, so be aware that Facebook will generally reduce the resolution of any higher resolution images. If you wish to include a higher resolution image on your Facebook business page, like artwork for example, you can first store the image online and then link to it on your Facebook page by entering its web address or URL.

Video Content

The last thing I wanted to share with you about Facebook content is what I personally use to create more organic engagement between my Facebook business page and my audience: Video. Why video? Well, video displays motion, which tends to catch the attention of your audience and really helps bring a marketing message to life.

Facebook set out to become the leading host in video views on its own platform, since before 2015, YouTube was still the main host of video views on Facebook. Once Facebook decided to do that, the first thing they did was spend $100 million on developing good video compression technology. They wanted to not only surpass YouTube in video views, but they wanted to deliver high quality and high definition video without the hassle and frustration of buffering. It worked, because in 2015, Facebook surpassed YouTube's close to a billion views daily and currently has more than 8 billion views per day on its own platform. So what's next for Facebook Video? Facebook now wants to be the leader in video views across all channels, just like YouTube used to be.

The main reason I like using video on my Facebook Business page is very simple and compelling for any business person using this marketing medium. Basically, Facebook will automatically deliver my video content to more people that like my page! Whereas written posted content may only be delivered organically in this way to less than 1% of the people who like or follow my page, Facebook will deliver my video content to upwards of 30% of these people! That creates far greater follower engagement with my posts and will ultimately foster much more business sales and growth.

What type of things do I show in my videos and those I recommend for my clients? Pretty much anything really, but I always remember that people buy from people. So that should give you the first clue to video marketing success, which is that either you want to be in the video yourself, or you want to have another company representative star in it instead. Make sure the videos are less than 30 seconds long, so a length of 20-25 seconds would be ideal. Also avoid putting text in the first three seconds of the video, although after that, you can include your website's address or a call to action written in text. Also make sure that the first three seconds of the video are especially engaging to your intended audience so they will continue to view it.

The majority of Facebook video views receive are without sound. Videos on Facebook play automatically without sound, and the majority of users will not change the setting to hear sound automatically when the video plays. Facebook reports that captioning a video increases average video view time by 12%, so that is a very important thing to keep in mind to help get your message across to more viewers.

You may also want to consider using the closed caption feature for Facebook videos, which works quite well.

To add captions to your video, follow this procedure:

(1) Click "Photo/Video" at the top of your Timeline.
(2) Click "Upload Photos/Video".
(3) Choose a video from your computer then click "Post".
(4) Facebook will then notify you when your video is ready to view. You can click the notification or the gray date and time at the top of the post on your News Feed or Timeline.
(5) Hover over the video, click "Options" at the bottom and select "Edit this video".
(6) Click "Choose File" below "Upload SRT files" and select a .srt file from your computer.
(7) Click "Save".

To add captions in other languages, just repeat steps (4)–(7) above for each additional language you want to add.

To remove captions from a video you've uploaded, use this procedure:

(1) Click your video to expand it.

(2) Click "Options" at the bottom and select "Edit This Video" from the menu.
(3) Click the X next to the file you want to remove.
(4) Click "Save".

Some of my clients use a newer smart phone to take their videos in landscape with the camera pointing sideways for easy posting to Facebook. With respect to content, they might have customers talk about their experiences with the company, its products or services. You could also show off your business inside and out or talk with employees about topics relevant to your business.

With today's technologically advanced smartphones — like Samsung Galaxy, iPhone 7 and that ilk — video quality has skyrocketed. I have an iPhone, so let me simply cover what I do with my iPhone and the videos that I shoot with it. Keep in mind that Facebook prefers that you directly upload your video to them. Also, your iPhone has a great camera and pretty good microphone. Nevertheless, the native app that allows you to take videos is not necessarily the best out there, and it will not maximize the functionality of your device. I use a downloaded app that really makes a tremendous difference in the video and audio quality of my videos. The settings are endless and the results are nearly as good as shooting with a high-end digital camera.

I see no reason to go through the many settings that are available, and you are probably just better off going online and then testing the settings that work for the purpose you have in mind. You will also want a tripod to help with camera stability, and you may want to get an app that provides better sound quality in some cases. Many add-ons for your smart phone are available that can really increase the sound quality, including the small, hands-free lavalier microphones that fit on lapels and are often used in television and theatrical applications.

Perhaps the most important thing you can do to improve your video quality is having good lighting. Find a place in your home or office that you can use for this purpose and add some lights to the setting. Lots of great options exist for LED lighting that you can find online. There are even some add-ons you can get for your smartphone as well.

Now that you have the equipment assembled, you just need to connect and turn it on. For me, I like to keep my video content short, so between 15 and 30 seconds should do it. I always tell my clients to just be themselves and to act as naturally as possible. Shoot some video content that seem relevant to your customers or prospects. It is even okay to just shoot an informal selfie video on the spot in many cases. I find that those videos actually work better than some of the pre-planned and professionally-produced videos.

As a recent example, we worked on a local county government election campaign. The candidate was late in announcing their run for office, so we had to get their message out to the community quickly and as uniquely as possible. We focused in on targeting the people that we know turn out to vote, and we then launched a relentless video content campaign aimed at them by posting several videos a day for three months. These videos were mostly short — even as short as 15 seconds — although some were as long as three to four minutes. Also, all of them were off-the-cuff and unscripted. The candidate would literally just pull over and shoot a selfie video wherever he was or if he felt that his constituents would have an interest in something or a situation he was in.

When we started the campaign, none of the other four candidates were using video, but within four weeks, all of the candidates had started using our strategy! The best thing to note from this is that all the videos were uploaded directly to Facebook, and the engagement between content and video from an organic reach standpoint was much more than what would otherwise have been achieved. In fact, more than ten times the amount of people engaged in a video versus the written content we posted. That was no accident because Facebook wants to be a leader in video, so they will promote your video content into the newsfeeds of far more people that follow you — all for free — than they will for the written content you post.

Basically, the sky's the limit, and so is the engagement with potential customers, especially if you hit a marketing home run and score a video post that "goes viral". This means that your video has become especially popular online and quickly spreads across the Internet as people share it on Facebook, via email or by linking it to their friends. Viral videos can thereby provide your business with a huge amount of wonderful and entirely free publicity.

Chapter 4: Anatomy of Your Facebook Business Page

Although it may only take a few minutes to do the initial setup of your Facebook business page, you will now find out about the many options you can use and the finer points you may need to become aware of in order to use your page optimally.

This chapter will start with the basics you need to know about setting up your business page and its two key images that you will need to provide to represent your brand. You will also learn how to create a custom URL for your Facebook page that is easy to remember.

The chapter will then progress into a discussion of each of the horizontal and vertical menu items that appear on your Facebook page, including what they do and how to use them to the benefit of your business.

Basic Facebook for Business

First and foremost, you will want to make sure that you are utilizing your business brand effectively on your Facebook page.

The number one thing I see businesses doing wrong with their Facebook pages is not fully completing their profile. Fortunately, this is the easiest thing to fix, so make sure you complete your profile 100%.

Fill out all of the information that you can. Nothing should be left blank. Be sure to include your business address, business hours, contact information, phone number, website, and both the long and short descriptions.

Once you have completed the above, you have now taken care of the basics. The following sections of this chapter cover the additional finer points you should address when setting up your business Facebook page.

I certainly do more than this for my clients, but I wanted to make sure I hit all the high points for you to provide a beginner's road map of what you will need to be accomplishing on Facebook for your business.

Page Likes

Facebook allows visitors to "Like" business pages by pressing a button near the top of the page to indicate they do so. This button appears immediately under the cover photo image, at the leftmost side of the horizontal row of buttons situated there.

This "Like" feature lets you connect with all the people who can make a difference to your business' success. It can also show new visitors how many other people currently support your business by liking it.

Page Follows and See First

In addition to liking a Facebook business page, a visitor can also elect to follow that page in order to have the posts made to that page appear in their personal News Feed.

People will also automatically follow business pages that they have already liked by using the "Like" feature, although they can follow a business page without choosing to "Like" the page.

A useful thing to tell your most loyal clients is that they can select your Facebook page posts to be among those they "See First" in their News Feed. This means that your page's posts, as well as those of other pages or people they have highlighted in this way, will appear at the top of their News Feed.

They can choose up to 30 pages or people to "See First" in this manner by going to their "News Feed preferences", and performing the following steps:

(1) Click on "Prioritize who to see first"

(2) Select a person or page to see first.

They can also use the "See First" function from a business page by following this sequence of steps:

(1) If not already following the page, click on the "Follow" button under the cover photo.

(2) Hover over "Following" or "Liked" near the page's cover photo.

(3) Select "See First".

Verifying Pages

One of the key questions I ask every one of my clients about their Facebook pages is: "Is your page verified?"

THE ULTIMATE FACEBOOK LEAD MACHINE

When you browse around Facebook, you will notice that some of the pages you visit have a check mark next to the title inside the cover photo. This indicates the page has been verified.

Facebook uses two types of check marks or badges to show people that the page is created and maintained by an authentic source. The first of the two check mark types or badges on a Facebook business page or profile is blue, which means that Facebook has confirmed that the page or profile is authentic for this public figure, media company, or brand. The second type of check mark that you will see on a page is a grey badge, which signifies that Facebook has confirmed it is an authentic page for the specific business or organization it appears to represent.

The following image is from my Facebook business page, and it shows I have verified it by the presence of a grey check mark next to my business name "DNApulse".

The above image shows what my Facebook page looked

like before the page formatting change, and the image below is what my page looks like now. Try not to worry if you notice that the Facebook page has undergone a considerable change, since they are always making adjustments, so that is worth getting used to.

When you look at the image of my Facebook page shown above, you will see the word DNApulse and a grey badge consisting of a white check mark within a circle with a grey background directly to the right of that text and just beside my smaller profile image. This verification is what we want to accomplish for your Facebook page, so it is the first thing I look for when I am qualifying a new potential client. If I see this badge, I know that someone who set it up has knowledge of how Facebook works. Furthermore, the business may also have had a Facebook consulting agency assist them with their page.

To be eligible for the grey badge, your page's category will need to be set to "Local Businesses or Companies & Organizations." If you are the admin for your Page, it has a profile picture, a cover photo and words above each image, and if you are eligible for the badge, you will see this option in your page's Settings.

To verify your page, you can either use your business' publically listed phone number or a business document like a telephone bill with your business' name on it. Facebook will use this information only to verify your Page with.

Follow this procedure to verify your Facebook page:

(1) Click "Settings" at the top of your page.
(2) From the "General" menu, click on "Page Verification".
(3) Click "Verify this Page", then click "Get Started".
(4) Enter a publicly listed phone number for your business, your country and language.
(5) Click "Call Me Now" to allow Facebook to call you with a verification code.
(6) Retrieve the code, then enter the 4-digit verification code, and click "Continue".

If you are unable to verify your page with the phone number, or if you prefer to verify your Page with a business document, then follow the steps above and click "Verify this Page with documents" instead at the bottom left of the window that appears. You can then upload a picture of an official document showing your business' name and address.

After Facebook receives your verification code or business document, they will then review your information to confirm that it matches public records. Facebook will send you a notification or email about your verification status within a few days.

You do not need to verify your page, although, as I mentioned above, that is the first thing I am looking for when I visit a potential client's business page. Yes I am something of an insider, but many people are now becoming very familiar with the verification badges, so I would strongly suggest that you take the time to do this yourself.

Also, as mentioned above, if your page represents a celebrity, public figure, sports team, media or entertainment company, you may be eligible for a blue verification badge. To see if your page is eligible for one, please visit the following link to complete the application:

https://www.facebook.com/help/contact/356341591197702

You also need to make sure when you are going through the verification process for the grey badge that your page category is set either as a local business or as companies and organizations. If not, you can follow the simple steps below to change the category appropriately.

To change your page's category:

(1) Click "About" on the left side of your page.
(2) Click "Page Info".
(3) Hover over the "Category" section and click "Edit".
(4) Select a category from the first dropdown menu, and then select a more specific category from the second dropdown menu.
(5) Click "Save Changes".

There is no limit to the number of times that you can change the category of your page. Also, if you do not see a category that describes your page, then please choose the closest available option from the categories listed. Once your page category has been changed to one that can be verified, you should then be able to continue with the verification process.

The deliverability of your content will also increase slightly through organic reach when you do this verification. We'll talk about paid and organic reach for your marketing efforts in greater detail later.

The following sections will discuss the two pictures you see on the top of every Facebook page. Those are your profile picture and your cover photo.

Profile Photo

A profile photo or picture is the small photo image that used to appear in the lower left corner of the cover photo. Now this image is instead situated in the upper left corner of the page and does not overlap with the cover photo. I would suggest using a profile photo that enhances your brand, such as an image of yourself, since people buy from people.

This profile photo is what Facebook uses to identify your page across many Facebook displays as a thumbnail image. If you have many Facebook pages that you are an admin or contributor to, then this profile photo is what those searching for you will see to differentiate between your various pages.

According to Facebook's current rules, a profile picture:

- Must be at least 180x180 pixels.
- Will be cropped to fit a square.

Here is an example:

Upload as
180 x 180

Shows up as
160 x 160

Be sure to take some time to create an attractive profile picture that will differentiate your business and represent it appropriately to existing and potential clients.

Cover Photo and the CTA Button

The cover photo is the large image that will extend across the top of your business Facebook page. You will want to use a cover photo that is formatted correctly and uses the right dimensions. Although your profile photo used to cover up the bottom left hand side of the cover photo, that is no longer the case.

My suggestion to most of my clients is to use a profile photo that has you in it — since people buy from people — and then make your cover photo something that creates a

Call to Action or CTA. You would be surprised at how many businesses miss the fact that the cover photo takes up 25% of the fold, i.e. the displayed page, so use the cover photo to drive home the offer or list-building opportunity that your business will benefit the most from.

You will also want to remember to use the CTA button in your cover photo. Page admins can select from a list of Call to Action buttons — like "Shop Now" or "Sign Up" — to add to the top of their Facebook page. The specific Calls to Action buttons currently available are:

- Book Now
- Call Now
- Contact Us
- Send Message
- Use App
- Play Game
- Shop Now
- Sign Up
- Watch Video
- Send Email
- Learn More

If you want to be creative and use something else, you can create a custom tab, which used to be situated directly under this CTA button and now lies on the left side of the page under the profile photo.

Most of all, remember to use your cover photo to drive attention. For example one of my clients gives away a free demo of their software on their Facebook page. They have an arrow in the cover photo that points directly to the CTA button that says "Sign Up". The cover photo also says: "1-click, 2-download, 3-free" along with a big red arrow pointing to the button to click. It's a great way to use what the majority of what people see when they first hit your Facebook page, which is the cover photo.

When selecting a cover photo, make sure to use the right size, and more importantly, the right format so that you end up with a very clear high resolution image. The secret here is to make your image **much taller than the recommended x 31 pixels** and 465 pixels tall, to be exact. This gives you 75 pixels on the top and bottom of the image that will be cropped on desktop. Keep in mind that with more than 80% of Facebook users now on mobile devices, you always want to check what your Facebook page looks like on a smart phone.

Below are the current recommended specifications from Facebook for a cover photo:

- Must be at least 399 pixels wide and 150 pixels tall. Loads fastest as an sRGB JPG file that's pixels wide, pixels tall and less than 100 kilobytes.

Here is an example:

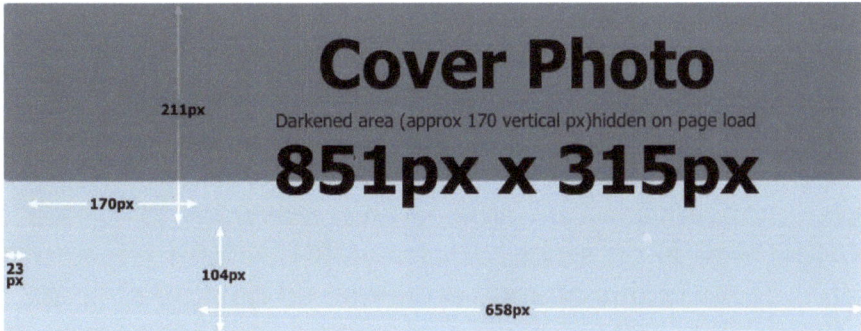

For profile pictures and cover photos containing your logo or text, you may get a better result using a PNG file.

Facebook automatically resizes and formats your photos when you upload them. To help make sure your photos appear in the highest possible quality, you can try these tips:

- Resize your photo to one of the following supported sizes:

Regular photos: 720px, 960px or 2048px in width

Cover photos: 851px wide by 315px high

- If you use a 2048px photo, make sure to select the "High Quality" option when you upload it.
- To avoid compression when you upload your cover photo, make sure the file size is less than 100KB.

- Save your image as a JPEG with an sRGB color profile.

Custom URL

After completing your profile, you will want to create a custom web address or URL for your business page. You can only make this change one time, so be sure to select a succinct URL that will always represent your business.

For example, my business page's web address looked like the following before I updated it:

https://www.Facebook.com/Dnapulse-75685459252191/

When I changed it on Facebook to a customized address, my URL now looks like this:

https://www.Facebook.com/Dnapulse

Do not miss out on this free opportunity to get a snappy custom Facebook URL for your business that is easy for clients and associates to remember. You can also put this URL on your business cards and website, as well as publishing it in brochures and other paper marketing materials so that customers can get the more timely and regular information from your business that you intend to publish on Facebook.

Facebook Custom Tabs

Facebook allows you to set up various customized tabs on your page that help you adjust it to be more appropriate for your business needs and objectives.

This set of horizontal tabs used to be located immediately under your page's cover photo, now they are down the left side of the page under your new cover photo location. They can be expanded to show all of them by clicking on the 'More' drop-down.

Tabs give you the means of showcasing custom content, along with the usual default tabs, such as "About" and "Likes", for example. You can also use custom tabs to provide visitors with access to any ready-made apps you may wish to add to your Facebook page.

Remember that the tabs you select to be among the top four or five should be the most important for your business, since only they will display the most prominently on its Facebook page. The other tabs will remain hidden unless a page visitor specifically looks for them using the page's drop down "More" menu.

Timeline

Your timeline is where you are going to make the majority of your impact on potential customers with the content you post regularly to your business Facebook page.

As described in the previous chapter, you can add text, links, photos and videos to your timeline that highlight and contain information your business' products or services.

You can also display some satisfied customer testimonials so that potential clients will feel more comfortable buying your products or giving your business services a try.

Events

Another great use for Facebook and your timeline is to post information about events that you are planning. This events feature can be especially helpful for performing artists that are looking to let their fans know about upcoming concerts, for example.

First of all, you will need to create an event listing on Facebook. You can then post it to your page's timeline and send it out to friends and followers to advertise the happening.

Such event listings typically inform people about the details of the event by answering such key questions as what, when, where, who and how much. You can also add a map and an event image.

Once your event listing is ready for distribution, you can then post it to your timeline and relevant Facebook groups, as well as send out individual invitations and manage the attendance list via Facebook.

People can then respond to those invitations to confirm their possible or definite attendance at the event, and they can also leave comments for you about the event, if you allow that.

The Voice Bar

The Voice Bar has already been discussed in an earlier section in detail. It shows up on a business Facebook page as a light blue bar stretched over the top of its Timeline under the page's Cover Photo.

An admin for your page can use this bar to easily toggle between either posting for the page itself or for their personal profile. This feature helps page admins avoid inadvertently posting or taking other actions on the page when mistakenly using the wrong voice.

Horizontal Tabs

The following sections cover each of the horizontal tabs appearing near the top of your business Facebook page above your cover photo and under the top blue bar. You will want to familiarize yourself with the functions it offers.

Page

The horizontal tab named "Page" will simply take you to your business page. It allows you to navigate there quickly from any of the other tabs on your site.

Your business page includes horizontal tabs below the cover photo that allow a viewer to "Like", "Follow" and select from the "More" menu. The "More" menu drops down to give the user options such as "Edit Page Info", "View as Page Visit", "Create Event", "Invite Friends" and "Share", as well as having an option for you to create an additional page.

The "More" drop down menu also has some additional items, which include the "Edit Your Review", "Block Page", "View Insights" and "Suggest Page" options.

Messages

The horizontal tab above the cover photo and below the blue bar named "Messages" will take you to your message inbox, where messages from customers or prospective customers can be accessed.

The "Message" tab will also let you filter different messages by the sender of the message or by flagged messages and labels.

Labels are created in the "Label" sub-menu, and they have two labeling options: "Follow Up" and "Important". Additionally, an ADD button lets users add labels for products, services, and to ask common questions. Creating labels and labeling items in Facebook messages allows a user to search by that label.

Notifications

The horizontal tab named "Notifications" accesses a page where different notices may be posted and searched. Notifications can be searched by "Likes", "Comments", "Shares" and "Other".

The "Notifications" page gives a summary of Activity with an option for Requests. Also, the "Notifications" page has the options to "Promote the Page", "Invite Friends" and "Be Shared or Suggested".

Insights

The "Insights" horizontal tab gives the user a summary of the Page's activity taken over the last seven days. The summary includes Actions on Page, Page Views, Page Likes, Reach, Videos and Post Engagements. The Insight page also shows the three most recent posts with the Type of post, the Targeting, Reach and Engagement. It also has a "Boost Post" button to promote the Page with.

The "Insights" Page has an Overview vertical tab menu that lists Promotions, Likes, Reach, Page Views, Actions on Page, Posts, Events, Videos and Messages.

Publishing Tools

The Publishing Tools horizontal tab shows Published posts with Reach, Clicks/Actions and the time that they were Published. The vertical menu here features Published, Scheduled, Drafts and Expiring Posts.

The other menus on the right side feature Videos, the Video Library and Videos You Can Cross Post, as well as Lead Ad Forms, the Form Library, and a Canvas menu.

Settings

The Settings horizontal tab gives a complete overview of the page with Page, Messages, Notifications, Insights and Publishing Tools on the top. The Settings Page's right side vertical tabs include: General, Messaging, Edit Page, Post Attribution, Notifications, Page Roles, People and Other Pages, Preferred Page Audience, Apps, Partner Apps and Services, Instagram Ads, Featured, Cross posting, Place Tips and a Page Support Inbox.

In addition to the right side tabs, the Setting Page allows

the user to edit features such as: Favorites, Page Visibility, Page Verification, Visitor Posts, Reviews, Audience Optimization for Posts, Messages, Tagging Ability, Others Tagging this Page, Page Location for Frames, Country Restrictions, Age Restrictions, Page Moderation, Profanity Filter, Similar Page Suggestions, Post in Multiple Languages, Comment Ranking, Content Distribution, Download Page, Merge Page and Remove Page.

Help

The Help horizontal tab is a drop down menu with three options: Advertiser Support, Visit Help Center, and Send Feedback. Each drop down option gives the user the ability to inquire about Billing and Payments, Creating Ads, Ad Delivery and Performance, Ad Account Settings, Ad Management Tools, My Business Page, Reporting and Insights, and Instagram.

The "Send Feedback" menu gives the user the option to Contact a Page's Administrator and Report an Abusive Page. There is also an option for Getting Help about how Pages work. This Page gives the user two options, one to report an issue with a Page and the other to give feedback on Pages.

Vertical Menu Links

The vertical menus on the left side of a Facebook business page give a visitor a concise way to navigate it in order to get more in-depth information on your business and its products and/or services.

The default vertical menu links consist of Home, About, Services, Reviews, Photos, Likes, Videos and Post. This menu also includes a Manage Tabs link and a Shops link.

Each of the different vertical menu links are reviewed in greater depth in the sections below.

Home – the Home Page vertical link will direct people to the Facebook page's home page. The Home page is generally where the public will first go when their interest in your business takes them to your Facebook page for some reason.

The Home Page gives a summary of Posts for the page and the Post Reach for each post. This lets viewers know how many people have viewed the posts on the page. You also have the option to "Boost the Post Reach" by paying for sponsored advertising. The default fee for this service is $5.00 for a limited public distribution of a post, but this fee will increase if you want to have the post promoted to more people.

"Website Clicks" shows the amount of people that have clicked on the page's listed website. It also gives the page owner the option to "Promote Website". Purchasing this promotion directs Facebook to attempt to get additional clicks on the page's associated website for a default fee of $5.00.

"Learn More" is where you can place additional information on the business. This option also has a button which will direct Facebook to promote the page and get more clicks for a default fee of $5.00.

About

The About link directs potential clients to the About page, where an overview of basic information on the business — such as its physical location and its products and/or services — can be viewed. Many business websites provide a history of their business and an introduction to the people involved in the firm in their About section.

Services

The Services link gives the page owner the option of listing all of the services provided by the business, as well as detailing how potential customers can access these services.

Reviews

The Reviews link allows visitors to the page to give their opinion on the business and its products. Visitors can rate the Facebook page from one to five stars, and they can write their review in a box on the link.

Reviews can be further examined using the Most Helpful, Most Recent, and Star Rating sub links on the Review page.

Photos

The Photos link allows the page owner to post photographs related to the business. The Photo section can also be used to Create Albums. This function allows you to open up different folders where related photographs of specific products or events may be uploaded and stored for organizational purposes.

The Photos link also shows the page's Cover Photos and the page's Profile Picture. An option to examine "All Photos" is offered on the bottom of the link.

Likes

The Likes link shows how many people have "Liked" the page, and this link also has three sub links. The first sub link is "People Talking About This", which shows who is talking about the page and what they are saying.

The second sub link is "Total Page Likes", which gives the number of total "Likes" garnered by the page. Finally, there is the "New Page Likes" sub link, which shows how many new "Likes" the page has received on a percentage basis for the current and previous weeks.

Videos

The Videos link lets the page owner upload and manage videos. It also lets them store videos in a video library.

As with many of the other links, a "Learn More" button can direct visitors to the About page, the Home page or another Facebook page to obtain additional information related to the video or videos.

Posts

The Posts link shows all posts made by the owner of the

Facebook page, as well as posts made by visitors to the page.

The Posts link has three submenus, which show the "Status of Posts", a "Photo/Video" link and a link for "Offers and Events" where special events and promotions can be announced.

Manage Tabs

The Manage Tabs link allows the page owner to make edits and other modifications to their Facebook page. This link lets the page owner configure Actions and Tabs for the page, choose Templates, and add or delete Tabs.

An option to turn on Default Tabs allows the owner to let Facebook determine which tabs will be the most successful for the type of page being edited.

The Manage Tabs link lets the page owner edit the Home, About, Services, Reviews, Photos, Likes, Videos and Posts pages, in addition to creating new tabs.

On the left side of the Manage Tabs page are situated a series of vertical menus that can also be edited. These menu choices include: Post Attribution, Notifications, Page Roles, People and Other Pages, Preferred Page Audience, Apps, Partner Apps and Services, Instagram Ads, Featured. The menu also includes Cross posting for videos, a Page Support Inbox and a Place Tips link.

Shop Section

The Shop Section is where the Facebook page owner can

display their products and offer them to other Facebook members, so this section is very important for many business Facebook pages.

Having a Shop Section on your page is a new feature offered by Facebook that is currently in the process of being gradually rolled out. As a result, a Shop may not be available to your business at this time, and the Facebook Shop feature is currently only available for physical products and cannot be used to market services or digital products at the present time. If you are not currently able to sell via a Facebook Shop for some reason, then be sure to check back periodically to see if that policy has subsequently changed.

Facebook currently does not charge you for adding a Shop Section to your page, and it allows you to sell products to your customers directly from your Facebook page. There exist a number of considerations to take into account when opening a Facebook Shop, the first of these being where in the world you happen to live.

If your Facebook page is based in the United States, for example, your Shop section capabilities and features may include:

(1) Product and product information can be uploaded with no preexisting product catalog having been uploaded anywhere beforehand. There is also no cap on how many products that you can upload.

(2) The ability to customize and curate your shop's inventory, thereby allowing you to divide your products into

different collections.

(3) Direct selling from your Facebook Page. Once your product list is uploaded, your clients can browse and purchase products from you using any device without having to leave your Facebook Page.

(4) Orders can be managed and marked as shipped, with order cancels and refunds able to be made without leaving your Facebook page.

(5) Get insights into your shop's activity. If you live in the United States, you can track the number of views, clicks and purchases for each product and how much money you have received for each of them.

Residents of the United States have two options for their shop on Facebook, they can either check out directly from the Facebook page when making purchases, or they can redirect customers to another URL address to complete the product purchase. To add a shop section to a U.S. based Facebook page that allows your customers to check out directly from your Facebook page, you must take the following steps:

(1) On your Facebook page, click on the Shop tab. If the Shop tab does not appear, click the Settings option on the top right corner of your page. You then click Edit Page from the menu on the left. You then click the Add a Tab button and click on Add Tab next to the Shop option. The Shop tab should now appear on your page.

(2) Check the agreement box for Merchant Terms and

Policies, then check the "I agree to the Merchant Terms and Policies" box, and click "Continue". You may be asked to input your Facebook password at this point for security purposes.

(3) Select "Check Out on Facebook" and then click "Continue".

(4) Enter the business' email and physical address.

(5) If you plan to use a separate email address to communicate with clients and receive updates from Facebook and payment processing companies like PayPal or Stripe, you must uncheck the "Use this email address for customer services inquiries" box and enter a new email address to use for customer service.

(6) You can elect to set your Shop up with either Stripe or PayPal. If you select PayPal, then click on "Connect with PayPal" to log in or sign up for a new PayPal account. If you already have a PayPal account, but it is a personal one, you will need to sign up for a business account. After completing this step on the PayPal website, click "Submit".

(7) If you already have a Stripe account, you must click the "Connect to an existing Stripe account" link and follow the steps listed. If you have not yet opened your Stripe account, click "Submit" and follow the procedure in the email sent to you by Stripe. If Stripe asks you for a company website, you can enter the URL for the shop section of your page. For example, this might read www.facebook.com/(your Page's username)/shop.

THE ULTIMATE FACEBOOK LEAD MACHINE

If your page is based outside of the United States, your shop will have fewer features at this time, although that may change in future, so remember to check back periodically. For example, your capacity to manage your orders will be limited. Also, while the upload products and product information feature will be the same, you can currently only feature a limited amount of products. You can still get insights regarding the amount of views and/or messages sent and received for each product.

Now that your Facebook shop has been set up, you can begin adding products. You can also add a section to your Facebook Shop that redirects customers to another website to complete their purchase by taking the following steps:

(1) Click the Shop tab on your page. If you don't see the Shop tab, take the steps outlined in the first step for U.S. residents listed above.

(2) Check the box agreeing to Facebook's Merchant Terms and Policies.

(3) Select the "Check Out on Another Website" option and press "Continue". You will include the website when adding products to your store.

(4) Choose the currency you will be using. Note that once it has been selected, the same currency will be applied to all of your products and that it cannot be changed unless you delete your shop and create a new one.

(5) Click "Save".

Your Facebook Shop is now ready for you to begin adding products. Setting up a Shop on Facebook is clearly a very important step to take for just about any business wishing to offer physical products for sale, so make sure to take advantage of this opportunity if you can.

Chapter 5: How to Use Your Facebook Business Page Optimally

The reality faced by modern day business owners is that many of their customers will expect them to at least have an informative presence on Facebook. To not have such a presence even indicates to some that you may not be a legitimate enterprise.

A business Facebook page is therefore quickly becoming a virtually essential part of the marketing arena for businesses. In addition to helping establish legitimacy, it can also be used as an easy way to extend your marketing efforts into the online world. Facebook not only allows you to share updates on your products and services with the people who really matter, such as your customers, but it can also help you to bring in new business leads.

Furthermore, using Facebook optimally will involve making attempts to engage your existing followers with interesting posts to promote repeat business from them, as well as encouraging new visitors to "Like", "Follow", "Share" or even write a review of your page. Ideally, you will want to convince new viewers to ultimately become customers of your business.

Basically, using Facebook optimally means you will want to do your very best to build a positive image on Facebook for your brand and to focus efforts on engaging your business page's readers so that they respond and feel motivated to revisit your page frequently. Also, now that Facebook has a Shop feature, you may even be able to sell physical products directly from your Facebook business page.

Making Your Business Easy to Find

Perhaps the most important aspect of managing your business' presence on Facebook is making your business page easy and straightforward for interested people to find. This key aspect of promoting your business on Facebook is especially vital when you are planning on using your Facebook page to generate business leads and attract new customers.

Given the time, effort — and perhaps even money — that you are probably now planning to invest into your Facebook page, you really do not want your business to become the hard to find proverbial "needle in the haystack" when it comes to interested people finding it via an Internet or Facebook search.

Instead, you want your business' page to appear right on the top in any searches for your business name and to be situated in a very competitive location when it comes to the results obtained when people search for your particular product and service offerings.

A Facebook business page can typically be located online by an interested person either by them searching for it on Facebook itself or by instead searching in one of the various major search engines like Google, Yahoo and Bing.

Understanding how such Internet searches work and employing them to your advantage is very important to your overall marketing success, and so they will be covered in the following chapter in greater detail.

One of the ways you can make your company easier to find online is to publish a steady stream of posts on your Facebook page that contain links to your business' blog posts, if you have a blog, as well as to other relevant pages contained on your company's website.

This not only helps the major search engines find your company more easily, but it is one of the key steps to take when effectively employing something known as Search Engine Optimization or SEO techniques.

By performing the relatively easy tasks of setting up a Facebook business page and posting links to your website on it, you will naturally enhance the overall number of links to your website appearing online that helps determine a website's ranking in search engines.

Doing this will enhance your website's visibility in major search engines, but it will also probably improve your website's traffic considerably as clients and potential customers click on those website links you have posted to the timeline of your business' Facebook page.

The Importance of Updates

Making an update to your business Facebook page is an important part of promoting your business to its followers on Facebook. Basically, if someone has liked or followed your Facebook business page, then any update you make to it will appear as an entry in their Facebook news feed.

THE ULTIMATE FACEBOOK LEAD MACHINE

By making regular updates to your page, it allows your business to get regular exposure to those people who matter to your business since they may provide you with future business or refer you to their friends. Regular page updates can also encourage viral marketing or promotion whereby your posts are shared with many people by those who originally receive them.

Both performing status updates and posting interesting and engaging content to your timeline count as updates for this purpose, and they will be distributed to those people who like or follow your page all be it to a small portion but we will discuss more of that later.

Another important function that Facebook page updates have is to keep your business page visible to those searching Facebook for relevant keywords. If you have not updated your page for some time, Facebook will send the page admin an email suggesting that they do so in order to keep their page visible to the general public.

Also, if you manage to engage your audience enough to have them comment on your timeline posts, then their friends will see your post and the comment that was left. This phenomenon can also help substantially with viral post promotion and can greatly increase exposure for your Facebook business page.

Finally, do be careful not to publish too many updates too quickly. If you make a sufficient number of updates in short a timeframe, be aware that Facebook has an algorithm that will group such posts together in your followers' news feeds. This can hide the later posts and make them effectively useless for promotional purposes in comparison to the initial post that leads the automatic grouping that Facebook actually transmits.

Using Your News Feed

Using your news feed effectively to communicate with existing customers and followers, as well as to obtain new business leads, seems to be a combination of skill, persistence and a certain amount of luck.

To use your news feed to encourage viral promotion, you will want to create engaging timeline posts that your followers are likely to want to like or share with their friends in a favorable manner.

In addition to getting a broader base of attention or reach for your post, that sort of positive engagement gives your business an especially powerful endorsement. It basically tells the friends and family members of the person engaging with your post that they endorse your business.

Studies show that an advertising post is fifty percent more likely to be remembered by a person if a friend of theirs is associated with it in some meaningful way.

Some of the things you can do to increase the likelihood of your posts being shared by followers include making them intriguing, humorous, informative or useful in some meaningful manner.

You can also encourage people to share your news feed posts as a thoughtful way to endorse your business to their friends, just in case they might need an occasional reminder to take this very helpful action.

Of course, the exact sort of useful content you might like to post to your news feed will depend on your business. For example, you can consider posting things to your news feed like: helpful tips, pictures, video clips, messages, and relevant informational content like a how-to article.

In addition, you can post about giveaways to your business news feed, which is a very popular way to increase your business' exposure and get meaningful engagement. Another way to get your followers' attention is by posting special event or sale announcements to your business' news feed.

Promoting Your Posts

The previous section covered many of the constructive and low cost ways in which you can promote your business on Facebook using posts made to your news feed.

All of those news feed promotional methods can be easily employed without spending anything other than your time, unless perhaps you are paying someone to administer your Facebook business page for you.

Of course, if you do not already have one, you may also need to invest in a smartphone to take interesting images and videos with to post to your Facebook news feed. Studies show that photos and videos are shared more frequently by followers, and they will help make your Facebook business page more colorful and engaging to its audience.

One key thing to keep in mind about such free promotional methods is that not all of your followers will see all of your news feed posts. This is not only because they might miss the post by failing to read their news feed, but it also has to do with Facebook's partial forwarding algorithm.

As mentioned earlier, the result of this is that Facebook does not forward all of your posts to every follower all of the time. For example, videos tend to be forwarded by Facebook's algorithm more often than photos, so videos typically represent a superior method of promoting your business and engaging followers.

Furthermore, if you have an important post that really needs to reach your entire audience, such as a key sales announcement for example, then you may want to consider investing in a sponsored Facebook post. Paying for a sponsored post will help ensure that more of your followers and the people they are connected to will notice the item in their news feed.

Promoting your posts by sponsoring them on Facebook will definitely cost you some hard cash, but it is fortunately fairly easy to do, and you will typically end up paying in proportion to how successful your outreach efforts are.

To start a Facebook post promotion for your business, first create a post on its page's timeline in the normal manner. Once you have created the post you wish to promote, simply click on the "Boost Post" button at the base of your post. A window will then pop up that will allow you to convert your post into a sponsored Facebook ad that will automatically appear as part of each of your followers' news feeds. Sponsoring a post can only cost as little as $5 to $50 a day, with the amount depending on the number of people you reach with it.

You can also lower the promotional costs of your sponsored posts by choosing to target a certain group of followers. For example, you can select to only promote your Facebook posts to those who have a particular interest, who fall into a particular age range or gender group, or who live in a specific relevant location you wish to target.

The popup window also contains a pull down menu that lets you adjust the total budget you are willing to spend on promoting this particular sponsored post. The more you wish to spend, the greater the number of people who will be able to see your sponsored post, according to Facebook's viewing estimates. For example, choosing a budget of $5 will reach an estimated 390 to 1000 people, while selecting a $10 budget will reach an estimated 1,100 to 2,800 people. Of course, this depends wildly on the audiences that you are choosing to target and can change based on many variables.

Furthermore, when you click on the pull down menu under Total Budget, you can also select a Duration for your sponsored post. This part of the interface includes 1, 7 and 14 day duration options, as well as the ability to enter a specific date that you wish to run the promotional ad until.

You can also select a payment currency for your sponsored

post, which will default to U.S. Dollars if you happen to live in the United States. Payments for paid promotions can be made in several ways approved by Facebook in one of their accepted currencies. They currently include the following methods:

- Credit cards or branded debit cards such as: Visa, MasterCard, American Express or Discover,
- PayPal, and
- Direct debit from a bank account.

In addition, Facebook supports a variety of alternative payment methods for those located outside of the United States, as well as some manual payment methods for certain countries and currencies. Note that the payment methods available to you may depend on the country you live in.

Adding Action Buttons

One of the best ways to increase the interactivity of your business Facebook page — and hence the ability of those who like and follow it to engage with you — is to have a Call to Action or CTA button attached to it that solicits a particular action from a page visitor.

Creating a Call to Action button helps lead people viewing your Facebook page to take actions important to the success of your business. Furthermore, this important and versatile Facebook feature has no cost associated with it, so it is therefore strongly recommended to include an action button on just about any business Facebook page. We have already briefly discussed the important CTA button, and it is such a key part of your marketing strategy that it will be brought up in many other areas of this book.

As an example of their possible use, you can have clients click a CTA button to book appointments with you or to buy a product. You could also link to your company's website so that a visitor could shop or learn more about something you wish to direct them to.

Also, since not everyone is using this useful Facebook page feature yet, a CTA button can help distinguish your company and give visitors the impression that you are sophisticated and up to date when it comes to your Facebook usage.

To increase the chances that visitors will notice and therefore click on your Call to Action button, experienced Facebook promoters often recommend the CTA button on a page be one fifth larger than the business logo displayed in your cover or profile photo.

Adding a Call to Action button to your business Facebook page is relatively straightforward and you can select among several different types of Call to Action buttons as follows:

- Book our Services
- Get in Touch with Us
- Learn More About Us
- Make a Purchase or Donation
- Use our App or Game.

As an example of how to create a button that will direct visitors to your business website, you would take the following steps:

(1) Navigate to your Facebook page and then click on the blue button that says: "+ Add a Button" and is located below the page's cover photo.

(2) Now look at the area that allows you to select among the available types of Call to Action buttons you can put on your page. Put your cursor over the "Learn More About Us" option.

(3) Choose "Learn More" from the menu that appears.

(4) Select the "Link to a website or app" option.

(5) Enter the URL of the website you would like to direct visitors to in the resulting blank. This will typically be the home page of the official website for your business, although you can choose any address you feel is most appropriate.

(6) Click on the "Create" button to finish the process.

After setting your CTA button up, you should also take a moment to test the function of your button to make sure it works correctly. You can do this easily by moving your mouse to hover over the CTA button with your cursor and then choosing "Test Button" from the resulting menu that appears. You can use the same menu to edit or delete your CTA button if you would like to make adjustments to it or even remove it entirely.

Chapter 6: Using Advertising to Promote Your Business

As a business owner, the value of advertising to create an expansion in sales and clientele can be a key element to your business' overall success. Leveraging Facebook Ads as a marketing strategy can not only increase your level of business activity, but it can extend your company's social reach with a rather minimal level of marketing expenditure.

One of the biggest advantages to using Facebook advertising services is that it allows you to promote custom ads and/or content that targets a specific demographic. The cost of the ads depends on how many people the ad reaches, as well as on the subsequent response and engagement the ad actually receives while it is being run.

Before placing ads for your business, you should make sure that you have a clear objective and purpose for the Facebook ad. You will also want to narrow your audience targeting approach in order to gain exposure for your business among the people that you actually want to reach.

Also keep in mind the purpose of the ad, whether that is for increasing sales of a physical product, for brand awareness, for event attendance or for video hits, to name but a few of the possible ad campaign goal options. Remember that each action taken by your audience has a cost to it, so make sure that you have formed solid and practical goals within your Facebook marketing plan before placing your ads.

Facebook ads should also be rotated regularly, in order to

avoid what is known as "ad fatigue", which is when people have seen the ad too many times and have stopped clicking on it. Once the clickthrough rate begins to decline for an ad, Facebook penalizes you by hiking up the CPC or Cost Per Click, which in turn increases the cost of clickthroughs, likes and comments generated by your ad, and thus affects both engagement and acquisition campaigns.

Facebook Campaigns

The type of ad campaign that you ultimately select will usually depend on what type of product or service you are promoting to your Facebook audience. For example, an engagement campaign might be used to promote a future event, while an acquisition campaign could have as its objective "acquiring" contact information for a new list of targeted people that want to hear about your business.

The most important consideration when starting a Facebook ad campaign is to have a clear goal for your ads. This means setting a measurable objective to achieve for the campaign, and having adequate funds necessary to reach your desired audience with your ads.

Remember, setting specific goals for your Facebook ads will help you achieve a better return on your advertising investment dollar. For example, if you are promoting a conference and are advertising to boost attendance, a potentially realistic goal of attracting 200 people could be set.

Furthermore, if you are selling a product, you could set a

goal of achieving the sale of 500 units of the product. Once you have established a specific business goal for your campaign, an ad strategy on Facebook can then be much more easily implemented.

To begin the process, you will just need to open up the Facebook Ads Manager and select an objective for your ads. When you first open the Ads Manager page, you will be prompted to select from either a pay by "Auction", which is a bid to reach your audience for the lowest possible price, or "Reach and Frequency", which has you pay a fixed price to predictably reach your brand's audience.

Once you have selected the method of payment, you can then select from among the three columns listed below and named: Awareness, Consideration and Conversion. For example, if your ad's objective is to send traffic to your website, then you would select the "Send people to your website" option under the "Consideration" column.

On the other hand, if your objective was to increase attendance at your online store, you would select the "Get people to visit your stores" option under the "Conversion" column. Other options available in the Ads Manager interface include "Increase your reach", "Promote your page" and "Get video views", to name only a few.

Facebook Ads and Ad Sets

Advertising your business is much like telling a story. Facebook Ads give you a number of different ways to convey your story to your existing clients and to your custom targeted potential customers.

THE ULTIMATE FACEBOOK LEAD MACHINE

Each of the following items can form an integral part of your Facebook ads, and they need to be carefully selected to optimize your ad's effectiveness.

- *Photo* – One of the most engaging ways to promote a product or service is by the use of photographs. Using photos gives a simple, clean advertising format, which can be complemented with inspiring text.
  - **Using photos is easy and Facebook makes it even easier with a very large and comprehensive photo library**. You can use these photos royalty free and should have no problem finding exactly what need to express your ads objective. The images are also already formatted for Facebook.

- *Video* – A video ad for your business helps engage the audience and often generates comments on Facebook. Video ads tell the story of your product or service and can be directed towards a specific demographic, perhaps targeting the best audience by age, location or specific interests.

- *Carousel* – This format allows you to include up to ten images or videos within one single ad. The carousel ad format allows you to highlight different products or services and show details on them in different pages. This ad format can be used in a number of creative ways to accomplish a variety of advertising goals.

- *Slideshow* – The slideshow ad format features video-like ads that use motion, sound and text to get attention and convey your story over multiple connection speeds and devices. Slideshow ads are easy to create, and you can use stock images available in the Facebook ads creation process.

- *Canvas* – Facebook Canvas ads are specially designed for mobile devices and consist of a blank space that can be used to tell your business' story. The ads can be composed of full-screen videos and images, Call to Action or CTA buttons, and text. With the Canvas ad format, people can use their mobile devices to swipe, tilt or zoom in on images, which tends to give them a greater feeling of immersion in the content. Also, Canvas ads load quickly, which is always an advantage when it comes to advertising to busy and hence potentially impatient customers.

Choosing Demographics

Facebook ads can be directed towards people that are most likely to be interested in your products or services. In addition to the enormous amount of people that use Facebook, the social media giant also offers businesses powerful audience selection tools for targeting the right audience to meet their business goals.

The more you know about your audience's interests and behaviors, the easier it is to reach then through a

Facebook ad. Facebook offers three options for choosing your audience:

- *Core Audiences* – The Core Audience targeting option are features that are built into the Ads Manager and Power Editor and allow you to reach people based on their demographics, behaviors, location, and interests. Selecting your audience based on demographics lets you choose the age group, gender, educational level, and workplace or job title of the target audience. The location feature lets you reach people in the geographical location you want to do business in. Selecting people based on their interests and behaviors sorts people by their hobbies, favorite entertainment, device usage and other activities.

- *Custom Audiences* – The Custom Audiences targeting option helps you locate your existing customers and contacts on Facebook. By connecting with your existing Facebook contacts, you can expand your relationships and help drive sales to those who are already familiar with your business. Custom Audiences can be made up of loyal and potential customers, visitors to your website or blog, and mobile device users that employ your mobile app.

- *Lookalike Audiences* – The Lookalike targeting option helps you find and connect with people that are similar to your existing customers and mobile app visitors. This option is created automatically from sources that you upload or connect to Facebook, and it represents a fast and efficient way to connect with more people that are likely to respond to your ads.

In addition to the targeting options described above, Facebook Audience Insights gives advertisers aggregate information on three key groups of people: those who are connected to your page via Likes or Follows, those who are in your Custom Audience group, and those who are on Facebook.

The Audience Insights feature gives you an overview of demographics and third party information on what products people may be interested in buying. In addition, Audience Insights uses income, family size, relationship status and location to determine the types of people who might be most likely to have an interest in your business and its offerings.

Engagement Ads

Facebook app engagement ads help you to increase the actions available in your mobile app. App engagement ads help you in reaching people that use or have your mobile app on their mobile device, so you can then prompt them to return and "take action" with "Call to Action" options.

With an app engagement ad, you can direct people to a specific area in your app such as the start of a game, a travel search or a product page.

The Call to Action feature lets you easily promote existing or potential client activity such as "Open Link", "Use App", "Listen Now", "Watch Now" or "Shop Now", to name just a few examples. The better your ad's Call to Action button actually fits your app, the more traffic to the app that can be expected from the use of the ad.

Impact Marketing

Impact marketing is an advertising approach that uses unconventional and cost effective methods to raise awareness about a company's product or service. Using Facebook ads to apply alternative marketing strategies can lead to extremely successful results.

In order to employ impactful marketing techniques using Facebook ads effectively, a very helpful initial step involves becoming familiar with your competitors. You can perform some initial research into the Facebook users that have purchased products or services from your competitors, as well as finding out which people liked the product and including their profiles in the target audience for your ads.

Other methods of impact marketing could be to post interesting or unusual pictures of your product, as well as quotes or other interesting items associated with your business. The key to using guerrilla marketing techniques on Facebook is to think outside of the box and to generate interest in a product or service by using something unusual to attract attention.

THE ULTIMATE FACEBOOK LEAD MACHINE

When running your ads, keep in mind that over 84% of Facebook use is from mobile devices, so you will want to make sure that your ads are designed to maximize your opportunity with that vertical. Facebook will automatically scale your images and text, but what you will need to do, is make sure that anything you are doing after the engagement with your ad — like driving people to a landing page or website — uses mobile-responsive technology so that you do not lose the customer's experience and access.

Chapter 7: How People Find Your Facebook Business Page

Although you may already have put hours of effort into creating an enticing Facebook business page to attract clients with, that time will not be especially well spent if you do not take some important steps to make sure that your target audience will be able to find your page readily.

Before you take any steps beyond what has already been suggested, you should first familiarize yourself with how people will be most likely to find your Facebook business page.

The following sections of this chapter will discuss some of the most common ways that Facebook pages are discovered by potential clients for your business.

Searching Facebook

Facebook offers its own internal search engine that allows people on Facebook to search for Facebook pages and members by entering a set of keywords, which are simply relevant words or concepts related to the item being searched for.

Access to this search engine appears in the form of a white field at the top left of a Facebook page situated inside the deep blue header bar. This field has light grey text inside saying "Search Facebook", and users can simply type the keywords they wish to search for and press Enter to commence searching.

THE ULTIMATE FACEBOOK LEAD MACHINE

When a set of keywords has been searched for using Facebook, the Results section listed subsequently might include such things as:

- Places
- Links
- Photos
- Videos
- Posts from friends and groups
- Public posts

Users can then browse among the results Facebook's search engine offers by clicking on the associated links. Note that each of these results will be links to Facebook pages, content, groups, profiles, places or posts.

Once you have set up your Facebook business page, you will want to make sure that your business is prominently listed in the Facebook search engine results when you type in its name

Facebook will also automatically propose a list of search items in a pull down menu when some words have been typed into the Search field. You would ideally like your business to come up there prominently as well.

Be sure to note that your profile image is the one Facebook uses when identifying your business page in its searches, so make sure that this key image is appropriate and designed to catch the eye of potential business leads.

Internet Search Engines

Internet search engines are software systems that help people look for information on the World Wide Web. The results of such searches will typically be presented in a list format with a link and a brief description of the website or item found by the engine.

Each item in a search list is also listed in the order of the rank given to it by the search engine that discovered it. The criteria used to determine these ranks are generally proprietary to each search engine provider and kept a secret from the public.

Internet search engines are used by the vast majority of people when they wish to find something on the Internet that they do not already have a specific Universal Resource Locator or URL address for. They also usually list relevant Facebook pages prominently, which is another great reason to have a business Facebook page.

The major Internet search engines include the following:

- Google
- Bing
- Yahoo
- Ask
- AOL Search
- Wow
- Webcrawler
- MyWebSearch
- Infospace

- Info.com
- DuckDuckGo

Although many more search engines exist than those listed above, the vast majority of Internet searchers will use at least one of the top three engines, with Google being the preferred search engine overall for most people browsing the Internet.

Given the importance of high ranking search engine listings for the exposure your business will get on the Internet, you must therefore plan on taking appropriate steps to get your business website and Facebook page listed prominently on relevant search engine listings, especially Google.

Getting your business' search engine rankings as high as they can be belongs to a field called Search Engine Optimization or SEO. Specialists in that field can take a variety of steps to help your website rank well among competing pages for the most relevant Google searches. They typically do this by making it as easy as possible for the search engine providers' spiders — which are software programs that catalog the Internet's content — to find and compile information about your website or Facebook page.

For example, an SEO expert might first of all make sure that you have a high quality website to offer potential clients. They might then edit your page's name and heading, as well as its title, description, alt and keyword tags to be relevant to the specific search keywords you wish to optimize your business' search engine listing rank for. They might also arrange for major and reputable websites to link to your website. They may remove Flash animation and the use of splash pages on your website to make it easier for search engine spiders to find your page. They might also post text content on your website that repeats the use of the specific keywords you are interesting in ranking well for. Finally, they can submit your website to the major search engines and add it to various online directories in the appropriate categories.

This is a great place to discuss SEO versus other types of organic and paid advertising options. This topic is very relevant to what you should do to promote your business online and/or the professionals you should hire to help you achieve that. Compared to SEO, Facebook advertising remains an important and generally cheaper advertising option when looking to engage a professional marketing firm like mine.

Most digital agencies want to get you on Google ads because they can charge you a lot more for their services. Many firms use all of these vertical advertising options, such as Facebook and Google Ad words, to actually sell you on Search Engine Optimization or SEO. Unfortunately, using SEO makes it much harder to close the sales loop and measure the overall success of this strategy. With Facebook and Google, it seems much more straightforward to run a campaign and track your leads generated in order to determine your ultimate return on investment or ROI.

To be clear, how to close the loop on your leads and turn them into sales is probably the million dollar question when it comes to marketing, and it is certainly the one I get asked the most frequently. With Facebook and Google, you first spend the money for a campaign, and you can then measure the success from the sales it generated. It can still take 60, 90 or more days to get a sale, but this is far faster than the results from traditional SEO techniques.

Furthermore, digital marketing agencies tend to like SEO because they will tell you that it is a much better marketing strategy since it will generate organic traffic that you do not have to pay for because it comes from people searching for your area of expertise or relevant content on the Internet. That may be true, but it is not free because you will usually pay a lot more for a lot longer with SEO just to generate the content that brings in those searches.

Digital agencies especially like SEO because it could take two to three years for them to get your SEO optimized. When you add up all the expenses it took over those years to generate that organic traffic, SEO seems far from free. The ideal situation is to create a balance of SEO and paid direct digital marketing via Facebook.

Facebook Business Page Suggestions

Facebook will automatically propose other similar Facebook pages when a user "Likes" a page, which is known as a Facebook Business Page Suggestions. Facebook apparently does this because it wants users to find and "Like" additional pages.

On the one hand, having this feature means that your business could be discovered by a new client in this way after they have liked a competitor's page. On the other hand, it means that a potential customer could be lured away to the page of another similar business as a result of clicking on one of these business page suggestions.

It is important to note that these business page suggestions are not ads that you can pay for to get listed more prominently. Facebook instead uses a listing algorithm that bases its page suggestions on pages with similar locations, category, and "Likes" by your fans who have either liked or followed your own page.

A viewer of these business page suggestions can hover over each page's thumbnail image to either "Like" it immediately or click on it to visit the page instead. They can also click on "See All", in which case they will be able to view the "Like Your Favorite Pages" browser.

User Business Page Suggestions

In addition to making suggestions when a user visits and likes a new page, Facebook has also started to make business page suggestions to those users who are making a specific post.

In this case, the user may get a list of Facebook's business page suggestions as they get ready to write a comment that responds to and mentions a page's name.

These user business page suggestions typically pop up for posts appearing on your Facebook page, so some businesses prefer to turn them off to avoid losing clients to their competition.

Since they are optional, user business page suggestions can easily be turned off by your page's admin in the page settings menu.

To turn off such user business page suggestions, also known as "Similar Page Suggestions" in the settings section, you can follow this procedure:

(1) Look at the top of your Facebook business page and click on "Edit Page".
(2) Select "Edit Settings" from the menu.

(3) Click on "Similar Page Suggestions".

(4) Uncheck the box next to "Similar Page Suggestions".

(5) Click on "Save Changes".

Although it is possible to turn these suggestions off, and that may seem desirable in some situations, note that turning them off means that your page will not be suggested itself by Facebook when posts are made on other pages.

As a result, you may want to leave them on — especially if you are looking to get more fans for your own business page.

Having People "Like" Your Business Page

Getting your Facebook Business page "Liked" by people will generally also increase your page's following, since anyone who likes your page automatically becomes a follower. Studies show that the more "Likes" your page has, the more probable people visiting your page for the first time are to also "Like" it and take your business and its offerings seriously.

You can start this very important "Liking" process out by inviting your own friends to like your Facebook business page. To do so, you will need to take the following steps:

(1) Hover over the word "More" situated below your page's cover photo.

(2) Select "Invite Friends" from the list.

(3) Click on "Search All Friends" to select from a list of your friends. You can also just enter a friend's name in the search box provided.

(4) Click the "Invite" button situated next to the name of the friends you wish to invite to like your page.

Furthermore, if you have especially friendly customers that wish to help your business out or to whom you have offered an incentive, then you can also have them ask their friends to like your Facebook business page using the same process.

Be aware that not everyone will know how to do this with Facebook, so you may need to be prepared to educate them on this procedure in order to make sure they can follow through on their promise to assist you.

Using the "Share" feature

When visitors or fans of your business Facebook page use

the Facebook "Share" function to copy any of its content onto either their own timelines or those of their friends, your business page can suddenly get much wider exposure.

Sharing content in this important way is how images and videos go viral on Facebook. Furthermore, getting shares can become an excellent source of free advertising for your business if you know how to stimulate it properly.

In fact, many business advertisers who use social media now focus more on getting content shares than on getting likes and follows for a Facebook page, especially after a business page is already well established and has a good existing fan base.

Basically, when creating posts and updates, you will want to naturally inspire your fans and visitors to your page to share your content with their own social networks, while at the same time mixing up your content with a variety of photos, videos, text and links. Fortunately, a number of ways to increase the tendency of people to share your timeline posts currently exist.

The first and foremost way to get your posts shared is to use an eye-catching image that tends to elicit a strong emotional response in the viewer. For example, an image you post could make a person looking at it laugh or cry. It could also depict something that makes a person say "awww" because it is just so cute and appealing. Getting this sort of visual and emotional engagement with your posted content tends to result in a greater number of shares.

Secondly, you will probably want to keep any associated message very short and to the point. Studies show that Facebook posts that are less than 80 characters long tend to receive almost a third higher engagement rates. This indicates that people are usually forwarding your compelling imagery when sharing your posts and probably prefer not to have much associated text coming along with it as baggage.

Another helpful tip when crafting your narrative message to accompany your post is to avoid using the first person perspective indicated by words such as "I" or "we". Instead, you can make your posts seem more universal — and hence more "Share"-able — by writing to make it sound like your text is coming from someone other than yourself or your company. Consider writing more generic phrases like: "How cute is this?" or "A happy thought for your day!" since that will tend to increase the number of shares your post receives.

With respect to text content, you can often get a good amount of shares by writing about helpful tips and useful resources of particular interest to your target audience and fan base. Another potential "Share" bonanza can come from eliciting timely support from your fans for good causes.

Furthermore, studies show that including a call to action in your post's text can increase the tendency of readers to respond and share your posts. For example, you can tell people to: "Share if you care!" or write something like: "Go ahead and share it." Commanding statements like these tend to get readers' attention and help elicit the all-important "Share" response that you are looking to receive.

Remember that no matter what content they are sharing, anytime someone shares the posts from your Facebook business page, they are doing you a favor by giving your business free advertising. It really takes very little time to thank them for this important publicity, so make sure to "Like" their shares and give them a smile or another short comment to show that you noticed and are grateful. Not only is this a common courtesy, but it could also help encourage them to share more of your posts in future.

Via Your News Feed

A user's News Feed is the list of Facebook stories that regularly updates shown in the middle portion of their home page. Their News Feed will typically include things like:

- Status updates
- Photo and other images
- Videos
- Links
- App activity
- Likes

This information comes from the people, pages and groups that they have previously chosen to like and/or follow on Facebook.

One key way of getting people to find your Facebook business page is to post items on your page's timeline that its followers may be tempted to comment on or share. These timeline posts become part of your Facebook page's content and can also show up on any of your followers' News Feeds.

The act of performing such actions is known among Facebook users as "engagement", and you will typically want to maximize the number of people engaged with your page in order to get the most exposure to potential business leads via Facebook as possible.

Basically, when followers do share engaging timeline content items like that on their own timelines, their friends can then receive a notification and a copy of the item in their own Facebook news feeds. This feature can help spread the news about your business and the offers you post on your timeline, which usually amounts to cheap commercial publicity since you have to deduct whatever it cost you to achieve it in the first place.

Sometimes an older story posted to your page will continue to remain at the top of your page's fans' News Feeds because a number of their friends have also liked or commented on the same post. This makes it important for you or your Page Admin to reply frequently to people who comment on your post, to encourage others to reply. You can also post updates on the post as well, since this also helps to improve its visibility in fans' News Feeds.

Some increasingly popular ways of encouraging engagement with Facebook posts include giveaways and discounts that can stimulate great interest in your page's News Feed. The small amount of money these marketing activities might cost your business are often dwarfed by the amount of favorable engagement they can generate for its

Facebook page.

The frequency and timing of your Facebook posts is another important issue you will want to address to maximize follower engagement with them. Most people tend to start to ignore businesses that post too actively, so it might be a good idea to keep your posting frequency to around once every couple of days, for instance. Studies show that U.S. based Facebook users also have a greater tendency to engage with posts made around 3pm EST and on Wednesdays than at other times and days, so you can also keep that in mind when choosing a time to release an important post.

The Events Listed on Your Page

A very useful feature of Facebook is that it allows you to create events associated with a particular Facebook business page and post them on your page's timeline and in groups. Organizing events can help create engagement with your fan base and generate business leads.

In addition to advertising events on your page, you can also use Facebook's events feature to share event details, organize gatherings, invite guests, upload photos, post and respond to posted comments from others, and receive confirmations from invitees about whether they can attend or not.

You can create a private or public event by following this procedure on Facebook:

(1) Click on "Events" in the menu on the left side of your

News Feed.

(2) Click on the blue "+ Create" button in the upper central part of your screen.

(3) Click on "Create Private Event" and then select from the drop down menu whether you want to create a private event or a public one.

(4) Fill in the fields in the resulting online form. You will probably want to include details like the: Event Name, Location, Start and End Times, Category, and Description.

(5) Click the blue "Create" button at the bottom right of the form.

(6) Choose a cover image to represent your event with.

You can later edit each of these items, except for the privacy settings, so you can either make sure you have entered that information correctly or just delete your event and start over if you made a mistake.

Chapter 8: Integrating Facebook Social Media Plugins

As the use of Facebook expands among the online community, the integration of its service with those of other mainstream, alternative and social media outlets has become widespread. Adding Facebook plugins to WordPress blogs has become especially popular, and that process will be described later in this chapter.

Other popular website hosting and development companies — like Webs.com, for example — include the ability for users to easily add social media plugins of their choosing to attractive web pages that they can even assist you in designing. They will also provide a free subdomain and host such pages at no charge — provided that you agree to display their advertising on them, of course.

More tech-savvy Facebook users can also employ the company's own Software Development Kit or SDK that is a set of software development tools that permit you to create applications for Facebook. Furthermore, many existing plugins are available to have your website interface with Facebook. Such plugins are a set of software components that add particular and generally desirable abilities to a larger software application.

Using Facebook's SDK to implement useful related plugins will require you or someone you employ to have the basic website development experience needed to incorporate the necessary HTML code that Facebook provides into your website pages.

THE ULTIMATE FACEBOOK LEAD MACHINE

The portion of Facebook's website that is aimed at developers contains specific instructions for incorporating the Facebook SDK for Javascript directly into your website's pages that will allow your business' audience to use its various functions without downloading or installing standalone files.

These Facebook SDK functions work on both mobile and desktop web browsers, and they include being able to:

(1) Use the Facebook "Like" button and other social plugins directly on your website.

(2) Let people wanting to sign up to your website to instead login to Facebook to accomplish that.

(3) Call Facebook's Graph API function.

(4) Launch Dialogs to allow people to perform useful relevant actions, such as sharing stories on Facebook.

(5) Make communication easier when developing a game or an app for Facebook.

The following sections will discuss some of the more popular Facebook social media plugins and why you may wish to incorporate them into your business website to get more exposure for your Facebook business page and help generate business leads as a result.

The "Like", "Share" and "Follow" Buttons

Perhaps the three most popular forms of Facebook social media plugins are the "Like", "Share" and "Follow" buttons. The first of these allows a visitor to your website to click on a button to simply "Like" the content and share it on their Facebook timeline.

The second popular Facebook plugin allows visitors to instead "Share" the relevant website content so that they can add a personal message to the resulting Facebook post and customize the list of people or groups that they share it with.

The third type of popular plugin involves adding a "Follow" button that will allow your website visitors to subscribe to the public updates of the person's Facebook profile you specify.

Unless you have a website builder that will automatically generate the required HTML code and add it to your website, you will want to perform the following steps to generate the Facebook Like button code and include it in the HTML code of relevant pages on your website.

First of all, you will need to use Facebook's Like Button Configurator form to generate the button HTML code. You should fill in the form's blanks that include fields for:

- The URL to like
- The Button Width
- The Layout
- The Action Type

- The Button Size

You will also see a couple of check boxes on the form that allow you to check them if you want to include friends' faces, as well as if you want to include a "Share" button beside the "Like" button you are generating HTML code for. You will usually want to include both of these buttons to help generate more fans for your Facebook business page.

Once you have filled out the form, you can generate the required HTML code by clicking on "Get Code". You will then be able to copy the resulting code and paste it into the HTML of each of the relevant pages of your website where you want to see the Facebook "Like" and/or "Share" buttons appear.

The procedure to add a "Follow" button to a web page is very similar to that detailed above. After generating the "Follow" button HTML code using the form Facebook provides, you will then need to add it to relevant web site pages manually.

The Comment Box

You can also create a Comment Box on your website that its visitors can use their Facebook accounts to enter comments into. The best part of this Comments Box plugin is that it also lets people choose to share their commenting activity with their friends on Facebook. It also includes moderation tools, as well as a social relevance ranking ability.

The process you will need to go through to generate the

HTML code to create a Comment Box for your site involves first navigating to Facebook's Comments Plugin Code Generator form. It has the following fields that you will want to fill in:

(1) Choose the URL of a website you wish to use the Facebook comments plugin on so that visitors can leave comments.

(2) Enter a width of the comment plugin expressed in pixels.

(3) Pick a number of comment posts to display initially by default.

You should then hit the blue "Get Code" button to instruct the code generator to produce the required HTML code for you to incorporate into each of your website pages where you want to see the comments appear.

Once you see the generated code appear, just select it, copy it, and then paste the snippet into the URL of each webpage as required.

Another option regarding comments that is supported by Facebook is to allow public post comments made by either a Page or by a person with a Facebook account to be incorporated directly into the content of a web page.

To do this, you will want to use the Embedded Comments plugin provided by Facebook. First, you will need to copy and paste the Embed Comment HTML snippet that Facebook provides into your target web page that appears online here:

https://developers.facebook.com/docs/plugins/embedded-comments

The next step requires you to determine what the URL address of the set of Facebook comments you wish to incorporate into your web page is. To obtain this information, follow these steps:

(1) Click the publishing time of the comment. For example, it may be "1 hour".

(2) Wait for the page to reload.

(3) Once the page has updated, highlight and copy the URL from your browser's address bar that should contain the string "comment_id=".

You can also get this embed code from clicking on the grey down arrow to the upper right of a comment and choosing the Embed menu option. You will then see a window pop up with the URL of the comment that you can copy and embed into your website.

Now just replace the data-href entry in the aforementioned HTML snippet with the comment URL you have just copied by following either of the two methods detailed above.

The Activity Feed

The Activity feed plugin shows the most notable recent activity that has taken place on your site. This might include actions such as "Likes" made by your friends and other visitors.

Note that Facebook currently reports that this plugin has been "depreciated" as a result of its release of Graph API v2.3.

The Live Stream

A "Live Stream" is a form of audio and video content that you can install on your Facebook profile or page. To have an event that you wish to use Facebook's Live Stream feature included on your Facebook Page, you can start the process by browsing to the following URL on a smart device that you can perform the live recording with:

https://apps.facebook.com/livestream/

Just hit the resulting blue button that says "Connect Facebook to Install". You will then need to go through the process of giving Facebook the authority to view and manage your profile information. You will also want to have a smart device available to record the live feed on, such as an iPhone or Android phone.

For Android devices, you can also run your Facebook app and then tap "Live", which can be found near the top of your Facebook news feed or page. For Apple smart devices, you will also want to start your Facebook app, and then tap the top of your News Feed or Page briefly.

At that point, you will want to follow these instructions for both types of device:

(1) Optionally write a description of your broadcast.

(2) Touch the "Go Live" button to start your live broadcast running.

(3) Touch Finish to conclude your live broadcast.

Live videos recorded in this manner will remain on your Facebook timeline or page just like any other video you post. Note that they currently cannot be longer than four hours in length.

Any "Likes" or other reactions that arrive while your broadcast is live will briefly appear on the screen. Also, a stream of comments will appear in real time at the base of your device's screen.

You can choose to block certain viewers during a live broadcast by tapping on the profile picture of a viewer next to their comment and then choosing the "Block" option. This process is reversible by clicking on their picture and choosing "Unblock".

This feature can be used to start a Live broadcast on your Facebook business page or profile that is also posted to your Facebook News Feed. Not only can you watch comments appear in real time on the stream, but you can also choose to make the live recording permanently available for viewing at a later time on your timeline.

Twitter

Besides Facebook, Twitter has also attracted a large

membership among the Internet's users of social media platforms. In particular, Twitter has become very popular as a way for celebrities, causes, businesses, educators and public figures to communicate frequently and briefly with their followers.

With respect to Twitter's terminology, making a post to your Twitter feed is known as making a "Tweet", while reposting a Tweet is known as a "Retweet". The maximum length of a Tweet is a mere 140 characters, although your Twitter handle and any media you include is not counted toward that. One of the things you can use Twitter effectively for is to Tweet to your business' followers about your Facebook page posts and WordPress blog posts, for example. You can also give them quick alerts and updates about your sales, products and services.

You can get several applications to help you communicate with Twitter that are designed to run on either your desktop or a smart device. Furthermore, you will probably want to link up your Facebook and Twitter accounts at some point. This will allow your Twitter Tweets and Retweets to post to your Facebook profile's or page's timeline along with your username, although note that replies made via Twitter will not be reposted in that manner.

You can perform this integration by following these steps:

(1) Log into the Twitter account that you wish to have associated with your Facebook profile.

(2) Go to the Apps tab of the Settings menu.

(3) Click on "Connect to Facebook".

If you are not presently logged in at Facebook, then Twitter will prompt you to type in your Facebook login details. Once these are entered, just click Log in so that you can sign into Facebook.

You will then see a page warning you that Twitter will receive certain Facebook information. To continue, just choose: "Okay". Then you will need to select among the privacy settings to determine who will be able to see your Tweets and Retweets that are posted to your Facebook timeline. This setting defaults to your friends. You then need to select "Okay" to allow your Tweets and Retweets to post to your Facebook profile's timeline along with your username.

If you want to link automatically on Twitter to your Facebook updates, then you can employ this online Facebook application available here:

https://www.facebook.com/twitter

You can then choose to post to Twitter from Facebook. Whenever you post a public update to your Facebook account, it will also be posted to your Twitter account.

If you want to connect your Twitter account to a Facebook page, such as a Facebook Fan Page or one you are the admin of — like a Facebook business page, for example — then you can post Tweets and Retweets made from your Twitter account directly onto your Facebook page. You can do this by following these steps:

(1) First connect your Facebook profile to your Twitter account as detailed above.

(2) Grant Twitter the "Manage Pages" permission for your Facebook profile by visiting your Apps settings.

(3) Also choose the page you would like to connect to in your Apps settings.

(4) At the resulting prompt, click to give your permission for Twitter to post to the chosen Facebook page.

Remember that having a more professional integration of your business' Facebook and Twitter social media profiles will tend to reflect better on your enterprise and provide a more consistent presentation of company issues, events and offerings.

WordPress Blogs

For many blog writers who use WordPress, the process of adding Facebook plugins to their blogs is fairly straightforward. They can usually simply instruct WordPress to include Facebook "Like", "Share" and "Follow" buttons whenever they produce a blog post to display on the Internet. These buttons can also display with counters that show how many times the article has been "Shared" and "Liked".

Furthermore, if you have a Twitter account for your business, then you can also include a button for visitors to

THE ULTIMATE FACEBOOK LEAD MACHINE

Tweet your WordPress blog posts to their followers. Another good idea is to integrate your WordPress Blog with your business' Twitter account by adding the Twitter plugin to the sidebar of your blog page so that readers can also view your recent Twitter posts or Tweets.

WordPress also has a very useful "Facebook Auto Publish" plugin available that was developed by XYZscripts. This plugin allows you to publish WordPress blog posts to Facebook pages and profiles automatically.

When using this "Facebook Auto Publish" plugin, you can choose to publish your blog post to Facebook in the following ways:

- As a simple text message
- As a text message with an image
- As a link that references your WordPress blog post
- By attaching your blog post to a post
- As a post to your Facebook profile page
- As a post to specific pages on Facebook

This WordPress plugin also allows you to filter posts by customizable types and based on categories. In addition, you can enable or disable the publishing of WordPress pages.

With respect to the available message format settings, you can choose to publish on a WordPress blog using the Facebook Auto Publish plugin with the following post elements:

- Post title

THE ULTIMATE FACEBOOK LEAD MACHINE

- Post excerpt
- Post description
- User nicename
- Permalink
- Blog title

Note that your "user nicename" on WordPress is very similar to your user login name but without including any special characters.

Chapter 9: Leveraging Technology

Once you have set up your Facebook page for business taking care of all the details involved and connected to your other social media accounts, the next step to take is to start to leverage Facebook's technology to generate more leads for your business. The value of Facebook to your business consists primarily in the broad reach of social media and its potential to help you attract new customers.

The value of being able to receive feedback from clients and the possibility of responding to customer's questions really is invaluable to a business. In addition, having a Facebook page for your business gives you the capability of answering customer questions and promptly clearing up any confusion about the business's products or services as it arises.

Remember, one of the most important features of Facebook is that people enjoy sharing with their friends and acquaintances when they have found an item or service of interest and value on the Internet. This is one of the great features about Facebook that can add significant value to your business page.

Some of the useful ways to leverage Facebook technology in order to improve your business are described in the following sections.

Leadpages

You can create Leadpages and publish them to your Facebook page as a tab. This allows you to cultivate your list right on your Facebook business page.

To create any type of new page or to edit an existing page, you can follow these instructions:

(1) Open the "Actions" menu from the pages list for the page that you intend to publish.

(2) Next choose "Publish Options".

(3) Then go to the "Other Publishing Options" tab.

(4) Click the "Add to Facebook" selection.

(5) From the Facebook selection menu, select the Facebook page where the tab is to be added.

(6) Click on the "Add Page Tab" option.

You should then be redirected to the new tab with your Leadpage now added to your Facebook business page.

When publishing a Leadpage to your Facebook page, Facebook will create an application tab image. The application tab image should be a graphic representation that best characterizes your business.

To customize the Leadpages tab, you will need to:

(1) Log in to Facebook.

(2) Click on the Settings menu in the upper right navigation area.

THE ULTIMATE FACEBOOK LEAD MACHINE

(3) Then click on Apps in the right hand of the Page Settings Menu.

(4) Once into the Apps section, press the Leadpages box in the Added Apps section.

(5) Click "Change" to add the new customized tab image.

(6) Once the "Change" option has been selected, hover over the image currently on the Leadpage.

(7) Press the "Edit" button which appears in the "Upload a Custom Image" box.

(8) You will then be able to upload the new image by clicking on the "Choose File" box in the "Upload Page Tab Image" box.

The new image should now be visible in the Leadpage.

If you are using Facebook ads, driving the ad traffic to a Leadpage can really help you boost conversions and lower the cost of your Facebook ads. By sending the Facebook ad traffic to the Leadpage, you can usually get a considerably higher opt-in rate if the Leadpage has been published as a Facebook tab.

Infusionsoft

Infusionsoft is a software product geared towards small businesses that can be used in conjunction with Facebook.

Infusionsoft allows users to organize customers and prospective customers with its Customer Relationship Management feature.

The software also gives business owners the ability to keep in touch with clients. They can also follow up with customers automatically through email and social media marketing. The program notifies the business owner when prospective customers are ready to make a purchase with a feature called "Lead Scoring". In addition, the software lets business owners sell their products or services online using e-commerce shopping carts, which are almost essential for Internet based sales these days.

Basically, with Infusionsoft you can share posts from your Facebook Page on your Personal Timeline. You can also create or update Infusionsoft contacts from the new business leads you get from Facebook Lead Ads.

By using Infusionsoft, a Facebook page owner can also add customers from Kajabi, as well as new event attendees via Eventbrite and Goto Webinar. The Infusionsoft all-in-one marketing and sales automation software really is a perfect fit to complement a Facebook business page and to help maximize its effectiveness when it comes to lead generation. That functionality also combines very well with its Customer Relationship Management tool, as well as its email and e-commerce marketing strategies.

AppointmentCore

The AppointmentCore software is a calendar based

program that lets business prospects and customers know when you are available to meet with them. AppointmentCore lets you specify what times you will be available for appointments by marking the calendar, and it also lets you display any times that you are unavailable to see clients.

The software creates "time slots", where people can see when you are available and then schedule themselves in for an appointment to see you based on your availability. Appointment openings can also be created at any time during the week or weekends, on weekdays only, or for a specific range of dates you can enter.

The AppointmentCore software can also integrate your calendar and availability with software offered by InfusionSoft, GoToMeeting, Google Calendar, and ConferenceCalling. Streamlining and automating your appointments and integrating that functionality with your Facebook business page favorably impresses newcomers considering doing business with you. You could potentially increase the rate at which the business gets new clients since the software is never too busy to take an appointment, unlike your telephone perhaps.

WordPress

The previous chapter has already discussed several ways to integrate your WordPress blog with your Facebook profile and business page. Remember, this will be an important part of your business' online presence, so connecting these very important information outlets is highly recommended.

Furthermore, as of May 2015, Facebook announced that they would no longer be supporting their WordPress plugin, indicating at the time that it would instead be maintained "by the community". Automatic, a firm that had helped develop the original WordPress plugin in 2012, stated that they were not planning on being part of the community support effort for this important plugin.

Nevertheless, WordPress still offers support for Facebook and Twitter, so you can post to WordPress as described in the relevant section of Chapter 7 and have your WordPress blog post appear on your Facebook or Twitter timeline. Blog viewers can also "Like" and "Share" your blog articles on their Facebook timeline.

Despite Facebook not supporting its WordPress plugin at the moment, there exist a number of options for connecting your WordPress blog to Facebook. An easy and efficient way to connect WordPress to Facebook is by using a plugin available in the WordPress plugin section.

The plugin is called Blog2Social, and it can be installed directly from WordPress. With Blog2Social, you can promote your business by automatically posting from your WordPress blog to Facebook and other social media platforms.

After downloading and installing the free plugin, the Blog2Social icon will appear on your WordPress Dashboard. One click on the icon will take you to the plugin's networks section, where you can connect your

THE ULTIMATE FACEBOOK LEAD MACHINE

Facebook account.

After installing the Blog2Social plugin you can repost, crosspost, and republish blog content from your WordPress page to Facebook, as well as to just about any other major social media website.

The plugin software gives the user two options to post: the first involves pressing the "Social Media Auto-Posting" button, which will automatically post your blog entry directly to Facebook and all other connected networks when you click on the Publish button according to how you have configured the profile settings.

The second option lets you customize your post, which can be convenient if you happen to write time sensitive or news related blog posts. The "Customize and Schedule Social Media Posts" option takes you directly to a preview dashboard where you can schedule when to post to Facebook.

Having a familiarity with your Facebook audience's preferences and how your WordPress blog relates to your business are key elements to take into account when linking your Facebook timeline to WordPress blog posts. Becoming familiar with your Facebook followers' habits and knowing when they tend to be online can also increase the outreach of your posts.

If you already know how to program, then an alternative method exists for linking your Facebook page to WordPress by creating a new App. While beyond the scope of this book, you can go to this Facebook developer's

The Ultimate Facebook Lead Machine - James E. Dicks, Jr.   178 website to learn how to do this:

http://developers.facebook.com

ClickFunnels

ClickFunnels.com features its website building software that allows users to create a wide variety of websites that help funnel sales your way. For example, these sites might include: lead generation systems, product launch pages, landing pages, sales funnels, squeeze pages, membership websites and e-commerce systems.

The following instruction set will show how to link ClickFunnels to Facebook:

(1) A tab link must first be created with ClickFunnels to Facebook.

(2) Once the tab is created, open your ClickFunnels account and click on the small Facebook icon at the right of the Home page.

(3) This will take you to a page where an "Add Page Tab" box will appear with a prompt to "Choose Facebook Pages".

(4) You then select the CF to FB tab from a drop down menu.

(5) Then select "Choose Facebook Pages".

(6) Click on the "Add Page Tab" button on the lower right.

(7) You will then be able to see the Click Funnel app on your Facebook page.

Hootsuite

Hootsuite is a social media management platform which supports network integration for Facebook, Twitter, Instagram, Google+, LinkedIn and YouTube, among others. Additional software integrations are also possible through Hootsuite's App Directory.

Hootsuite's user interface consists of a dashboard which integrates all of your social media accounts. Having everything in one place like this can significantly simplify managing your business' Facebook and Twitter activity. With Hootsuite, you can not only keep track of your Facebook business page and Twitter feed, but you can also use its tools to post updates, images and videos.

Another useful feature of Hootsuite is that you can monitor the reach of your Facebook posts, which you can track by region and language. In addition, the software includes "Facebook Insight Analytics", which lists all of the Facebook analytics in a comprehensive and readable report.

Furthermore, the Hootsuite Assignments tool lets you assign Facebook messages to your Hootsuite Team Members from your browser. Having all of your social media and business websites integrated on Hootsuite's dashboard could greatly increase your exposure to clients, as well as substantially improving your productivity.

To add a Facebook page to the Hootsuite Dashboard, you must first log into Hootsuite under the name corresponding to the account that created the Facebook page. You can then check off the Facebook pages or groups that you want to add to your Dashboard. Make sure you check the box next to the page you want to add, while the personal profile should remain unchecked. This will ensure that the desire page is added to Hootsuite, not the profile.

Facebook Global Pages

Facebook's Global Pages give organization and advertisers the option of providing localized versions of their content to customers situated all over the world under one universal brand name.

In addition, this Global Pages feature gives a Facebook user access to helpful features like their total fan count, a vanity URL and insights across the user's entire fan base.

Using Global Pages means an advertiser can choose to use unique content that is meaningful to a certain demographic in one location, while they can simultaneously display alternative content to a different audience situated in a separate location.

Facebook's Global Pages come in three different types:

- *Root Page* – This is an invisible page that overlooks the whole structure of the Global Page. The Root Page gives insights into all of the Global Pages and lets the user target specific markets with its "Add and remove countries" selection and its "Add and remove languages" selection options.

- *Market Page* – The Facebook user can have as many Market Pages as they desire. These pages can be customized and can redirect to other pages according to what language the target audience speaks and where it is located.

- *Default Page* – This is the page where the customer or prospect will be directed to by default if they do not meet the target market selection criteria that were set up in the Market Pages.

When people navigate to your page's web address or URL, they will then be redirected to the appropriate Market Page, if applicable, or otherwise to the Default Page.

To create Global Pages, you must first navigate to your Facebook Page and then follow these instructions:

(1) Go to "Settings" and click on the "Global Pages" tab.

(2) Select "Add a Page".

(3) Set the targeting preferences, including the country and languages that you want mapped to that Page.

(4) Click on "Save Changes".

Note that the admin of a Market Page can edit targeting

settings for these Global Pages, while the Root Page admins can edit targeting settings for all pages in the structure whenever they wish to.

Chapter 10: Facebook versus Google and LinkedIn

Choosing how to reach your business's audience effectively through Facebook ads is a very important element to their online success. Currently, Google Ads and LinkedIn are two of Facebook's main competitors in the online advertising realm.

All three media platforms have their own characteristics and reach extremely large audiences, with LinkedIn specializing in the professional sector and Google Ads offering their targeted ads over a large part of the Internet in numerous potentially interesting ways.

The following chapter compares the three different ad platforms, their advantages and drawbacks, and how Facebook Ads compare with the other two options.

Keywords are Limited and Expensive

The first thing to understand is how Google AdWords — which are Pay Per Click or PPC ads — drive business to an advertiser. The way advertisers use AdWords is that they bid on keywords that consist of words and phrases queried by browsers in the Google search engine. Those who pay in this way do so in order to have their ad appear in the search results.

If the person making the query is interested in the advertisement and clicks on it, the advertiser is charged a fee, which gave rise to the descriptive term "Pay Per Click". Basically, the bid optimization process allows users to pay for potentially finding new customers based on search term results and the keywords entered into the Google search engine. This advertising arrangement is also known as a "paid search".

While this method of reaching a wide audience has been proven to be an effective method of increasing sales, the auction system that Google AdWords is based on can become quite expensive.

The process begins when a user enters a search query. Google then determines whether the query entered by the user contains keywords currently being bid on by advertisers. If other advertisers have a bid on keywords contained in the user's search query, the auction for the ad begins. Google then determines the Ad Rank or where the ads will be placed according to a formula based on the maximum bid and Quality Score.

The Quality Score is a metric that determines how useful or relevant your ad is to the target audience. The higher the Quality Score, the better. Once your Ad Rank and Quality Score have been calculated, Google then uses the data to determine your ad's Price Per Click or PPC value.

The average cost per click in Google AdWords is between $1.00 and $2.00 on their search network. AdWords users are able to exercise tight controls over how their AdWords budget is spent and typically use different targeting techniques to reach the best audience for their product or service. Nevertheless, large retail corporations spend as much as $50 million annually for their paid searches on AdWords with the most expensive keywords costing as much as $50 per click.

The cost of using AdWords for small businesses currently tends to average about $9,000 to $10,000 per month on Google paid search campaigns, which is an extremely high amount compared to the cost of ads on Facebook. Even though advertising on Facebook alone can be less expensive, using Google and Facebook in combination seems to be the most efficient way to reach a larger audience to inform about your business and generate leads.

To get the optimal return on your advertising investment dollar, using the two platforms could be the best solution, but would typically necessitate a dual strategy to get the most out of each platform. Combining Google's "paid search" with Facebook's "paid social" is probably the most powerful advertising and marketing tool currently available on the Internet.

Facebook Ads are Cheap

While Google AdWords can help your business find new customers, Facebook Ads — or "paid social" — tends to help new customers find you. The biggest difference between the two platforms is that Google AdWords helps businesses find new customers through keywords, while Facebook Ads helps users find businesses according to the user's interests and their online behavior.

Google AdWords has become the dominant force in the online advertising business; although Facebook Ads have pioneered the realm of paid social media advertising and have become a central part of many businesses' online marketing and advertising strategy. Also, Facebook's audience rivals Google's, with a current market segment of roughly 2 billion monthly active users.

The value of Facebook Ads, in addition to the fact that they are much more affordable, is the considerable efficiency with which Facebook targets users and your potential ad audience. Because of the amount of detail that Facebook users submit to the platform, the opportunities for tailoring advertising messages to a targeted audience are unprecedented in their effectiveness.

Facebook also uses an auction method to determine the cost of ads. Basically, an auction takes place when someone is able to see the ad. The auction "participants" are ads targeted to the audience in which the eligible person is classified.

The winning ad is typically the one with the highest "total value", which is a combination of the three following elements and is not necessarily the ad with the highest budget:

(1) *The Advertiser Bid* – This is a bid that you set during the ad set's creation and can be either manual or automatic. The automatic bid is made by Facebook on an auction to auction basis and is calculated according to getting you the best results possible in spending your entire budget. This option is best for people without a specific value in mind for

the result that is being optimized or is still evaluating the right manual bid.

The manual bid is set by the maximum amount that you are willing to pay for the results for which your set of ads is optimized for. Facebook recommends that you set your bid at less than the maximum. If you win the auction, you get charged the minimum amount that would have been required to win your advertiser bid at auction, which generally means that you will more than likely be charged less than your bid. Underbidding is not recommended due to the fact that you may lose auctions that you would have otherwise won at no additional cost.

(2) *Quality and Relevance of the Ad* – Facebook represents how interested they think a person will be in seeing your ad measuring its relevance and quality, which can be gauged by checking the ad's relevance score.

(3) *Estimated Action Rates* – This is a metric that measures how likely the person viewing the ad will be to take actions required to get the results for which you optimized. For example, if you are running an ad for sports equipment optimized for purchase conversions, then your targeting will be directed to people interested in playing sports. Keep in mind that the relevance of sporting equipment to a person's interest does not necessarily mean that they will make a purchase. Therefore, Facebook searches from a pool of people interested in sporting equipment to find the people most likely to complete a purchase.

Basically, Facebook makes it easier to display your ad to people interested in sporting equipment and are likely to make a purchase based on the person's previous actions and your ad's previous performance.

According to third party data compiled in 2016's third quarter, the average Cost Per Click or CPC of Facebook Ads was $0.2729 per click and $0.2740 for all objectives. The average cost per 1,000 impressions or CPM in 2016's third quarter was $7.19 with $7.34 for all objectives.

The average Cost Per Click determined by objective was as follows:

- Impressions - $0.29 per click
- Link Clicks - $0.10 per click
- Offsite Conversions - $0.34 per click
- Lead Generation - $0.69 per click
- Reach - $1.04 per click

As the above figures clearly illustrate, the Cost Per Click for Facebook Ads generally seems considerably less expensive than Google AdWords.

LinkedIn Ads are Expensive

LinkedIn Ads can be an excellent way to target people based on their employers and job titles. Nevertheless, LinkedIn cannot offer the focused targeting abilities for your ads that Facebook can.

Despite LinkedIn launching a conversion tracking pixel in the second half of 2016, gauging your ad's performance on LinkedIn could still be problematic. Conversely, Facebook Ads have greater traffic volumes, much better targeting abilities and more variety in the types of ads you can choose. In addition, Facebook's optimization algorithm scales your campaigns to keep them at their highest level of efficiency.

The cost of LinkedIn ads is also a major factor to consider. LinkedIn offers two ways to control your ad campaign's costs: Setting budgets, where you specify the maximum amount you wish to spend per day, and Setting bids, which allows you to budget for each click of 1,000 impressions.

The two bidding options are Pay per click or CPC, where you specify the maximum amount that you wish to pay per click per day, and Pay per 1,000 impressions or CPM, in which you specify the set cost for each 1,000 times your ad is shown regardless of the amount of clicks. The minimum CPC or CPM bid for Sponsored Content varies depending on the targeted audience.

Basically, the minimum costs to advertise in LinkedIn's campaign manager are:

- $10.00 Daily Budget per campaign
- $2.00 Minimum bid for CPC or CPM
- $10.00 total budget, which is an optional feature for Sponsored Content

LinkedIn determines how often your ad is displayed according to the performance history of your campaign. Once you have depleted your credit, you are then billed periodically depending on the amount of activity your campaign attracts.

Google Trying to Catch Up With Facebook

With the 2014 release of Facebook's Atlas, a cross platform, web wide ad platform, Facebook has claimed a significant part of Google's multi-billion dollar ad platform. The new cross platform web wide ad platform is what is known as "people based marketing", also known as advance audience targeting and offers a number of beneficial elements for marketers.

The Atlas platform has enhanced tracking capabilities, with the user's ad interactions directly linked to their Facebook accounts, letting you keep track of ad interactions across all third party websites, apps and mobile devices.
The cross platform targeting options target online ads to specified users based on their Facebook interests, likes, preferences and demographics across all third party apps and websites.

The First Click Attribution Tracking option allows you to track what type of device was used on your customer's first click on your ad. The option allows your customers to make purchases of your products from a desktop computer even though they originally clicked on the product using a mobile device.

Atlas allows Facebook users to track Online to Offline transactions. For example, if a customer buys a product in a physical store and gives the store their email address, Facebook can then use this email address to determine where and when the customer saw your ad online. Nevertheless, the customer's email address must be connected to their Facebook account for this option to track data.

People Search for Solutions on Google

While people tend to use Google to solve problems or query information, Facebook users tend to look for products or solutions based on their interests and online behavior.

Facebook Audience Insights lets you access aggregate information on three groups of people: people in your Custom Audience, people connected to your page and people on Facebook. This allows you to create ad content that resonates with a particular demographic and helps you find more people that have similarities to your current audience.

Google, on the other hand uses keywords to drive traffic to your ad, which can be considerably more expensive than using Facebook Ads. The advantages of using Facebook Ads over Google AdWords can be significant depending on the type of business or service you are promoting, and could be considerably less expensive.

On Facebook, You Know Who Wants the Solution

The biggest advantage Facebook has over Google for advertising is that on Facebook, you become aware of who is searching for solutions, while with Google Ads people need to locate your business after a search, and then your ad must be compelling enough for them to click on it, which still does not necessarily end with a sale.

With Facebook Ads, your business is being searched for by people that have already expressed interest in your type of products by their previous searches and online conduct. The likelihood of making a sale or the successful promotion of a product or event is more cost effective and less complicated using Facebook Ads.

Chapter 11: Why You Should Be Advertising on Facebook

In addition to being one of the most affordable online ad platforms for your business, Facebook Ads have an incredible reach, with Facebook's 2 billion users and half a billion Instagram accounts.

Due to the fact that people share so many details about themselves on Facebook, your ads can be targeted to a wide audience based on their age, hobbies, location or any other search parameter.

Facebook Ads' targeting features are also by far the most sophisticated and far reaching for the money when compared to advertising using Google AdWords or LinkedIn.

Your Audience is on Facebook

The beauty of Facebook Ads is that in using their targeting features, your audience can be reached by:

- *Location* – Regardless of where in the world you wish to market your products or services, Facebook Ads can be targeted to specific countries, communities, cities and regions.

- *Interests* – Whether your audience consists of golfers or amateur photographers, Facebook allows the advertiser to target the audience based on their interests or hobbies.

- *Behavior* – Your audience can be selected based on people's purchasing behavior, usage of a particular device or other activity. For example, if your business was selling sporting goods, you could target people who have recently purchased sporting goods online.

- *Demographics* – The audience that will most likely purchase products or services from your business could be made up of people of a certain age, gender, and job title or relationship status, which can be targeted efficiently using Facebook Ads.

- *Connections* – This targeting feature allows you to reach people that are connected to your Facebook Page, an event or app and can be excluded to find new audiences. For example, if your objective is to get more likes on your page, people that have already liked your page can be omitted.

In essence, using Facebook Ads will allow you to locate and target a niche audience based on what those people are interested in and what they are discussing. Once you have an audience targeted, that audience is more likely to search out your product or service because they will already have an interest in your product based on the search parameters.

Scalability

To successfully scale your Facebook ads, combining many small successes seems to work best. Basically, having 100 ad sets at $5 per set that work well is a start. Once you see the results you desire, you can try increasing your daily budget. Be aware that increasing your budget and duplicating campaigns will often not yield the same results.

As you increase your daily budget, your cost per click will increase as well, adding to your overall expense. While the cost may be justified with increased business, increasing your budget in small increments makes the most sense.

App installs are the only off-Facebook conversion event that can be purchased with Cost per Action or CPA bidding. CPA bidding for app installs has been giving many brands positive results. You can easily determine how different CPA bids change the level of your daily spending.

Monthly and Daily Budget

Your Monthly Budget is the amount that you are willing to pay to have your ad sets shown over the month. A monthly budget can be set for each ad set you create. Keep in mind that you are not purchasing ads or the ability to display ads, but are informing Facebook on how much you are willing to spend to have them show your ads to people in your targeted audience to obtain the results you desire.

In addition to the monthly budget, the Daily Budget is the average amount that you are willing to spend on an ad set on a daily basis, and the Lifetime Budget, which is the amount you are willing to spend over the duration of the ad set.

Can be Huge (2 Billion Users)

When Facebook has "delivered" your ad, this means that they have shown your ad to the people from your target audience that are most likely to give you the result for which your ad set is optimized. Of course, with 2 billion users, you can have a huge targeted audience and spend an enormous amount of money on your ad sets. Facebook has two delivery types: standard and accelerated, which can affect how they spend your budget.

Standard delivery will have Facebook deliver your ads and spend your budget evenly over the course of your campaign, which is called "pacing". Pacing provides you with as much value as possible during the course of your ad campaign within your budgetary constraints and in line with market dynamics. Facebook will lower your bid at certain times to maximize value.

With Accelerated delivery, Facebook delivers your ads (and spends your budget) as quickly as possible, which means that they prioritize speed over efficiency when deciding on who and when to show your ads to. This type of delivery would work for a time sensitive product or an event, which would add value getting the ad out in a short time period.

Spend to Diminishing Point of Return

Reaching a point of diminishing returns typically happens when the frequency of your Facebook ad is high and more people than you expected are seeing the ad. Depending on the quality of the content in your ad, and how people react to it, your Facebook fans could increase considerably.

Remember, using Facebook ads is not just about getting more business, but about creating engagement. People will become more interested in your product or service and like and share it with their friends if they find the material engaging. Using Facebook Live is an excellent way to reach an audience of potential customers.-

The reason for spending to the point of diminishing returns on Facebook ads is primarily to monetize an audience and produce increased revenues through strategic business building. Nevertheless, the bottom line is that the wider the audience you are reaching, the more value you can provide with your product or service.

A/B Testing

Also known as split testing, A/B testing is a method to determine which ad headlines, images, body copy, call to actions or any combination of them work best to market your product or service to your audience.

If you are not experienced in creating Facebook Ad campaigns, then knowing what ad design would work best for your product or service or which demographic to target could be challenging. A/B testing allows you to test and compare multiple ad designs and target audiences to determine which ones would be more efficient for your goals.

THE ULTIMATE FACEBOOK LEAD MACHINE

In an A/B test, two ads are displayed side by side, underneath the ad graphics are two columns under each ad comparing the number of impressions observed, the number of clicks the ad generated, how many sales were made as a result, the money spent, and finally the cost per sale.

The higher the cost per sale, the less effective the ad is performing on the same budget. The advantage of the A/B test is clear and can save you a lot of money knowing the type of ad that will attract the most interest. A/B testing is most efficient for ad design, which includes title, placement, landing page, text, image, link description and call to action.

Targeting possibilities using the A/B test include location, language, gender, age, specific interests, relationship status and behaviors. Advanced demographic comparisons can be made based on family composition, household income, education, mobile devices and work title to name just a few.

The cost of running an A/B test can vary. The best way to determine the cost of an A/B test for your ads would be to first create a small CPC or CPM campaign with no tests to get an average Cost per Conversion. Once you have determined the Cost per Conversion you can then set up a split test.

You should allocate a sufficiently large budget to allow for at least 20 conversions per ad, to accurately determine which of the two ads will perform better for you. Therefore, if your test is for five images at a cost per conversion of $2.00, then you would need a budget of $200 or $2 X 5 images X 20 = $200.

What's important when A/B testing is to optimize your campaign fast with a minimum of tests, which adds expense to your campaign. Start small, testing only a few elements and giving them an adequate budget.

The Targeting Capabilities of Facebook Are Exceptional

Targeting an audience with Facebook Ads is one of the biggest selling points for Facebook. From targeting a Core Audience by location, demographics, their interests or their online behavior, to targeting a Custom Audience of people you already know such as loyal customers, visitors to your website and mobile users that see your ad, Facebook Ads is the most cost efficient and effective way to grow your business.

The Lookalike Audience targeting feature allows you to target people with similar behavior patterns and tastes as your current audience. The Lookalike Audience is created automatically from sources that you have uploaded or connected to via Facebook and is a fast and efficient way to connect with more people that would potentially be interested in your product or service.

Facebook Is Effective to Push On-the-Fence Leads Down the Sales Funnel

Facebook Ads and ads online in general have an average

website conversion rate of around one to three percent, which means that 97 to 99 percent of visitors are not yet ready to make a purchase or are "on the fence". With a conversion rate that low, the question is how to make the 97 to 99 percent of visitors purchase a product or service.

The answer is by creating demand, which can be accomplished by creating awareness of your product or service and make them realize there is a need. Once the need for the product has been identified by the target audience, they can then consider whether they want to make a purchase after researching potential options.

If you can provide something of interest or value, now is the time to attract the potential customer. After researching the different options, the potential customer will make a decision on the best choice. Your pricing, offers and other promotions that you may be conducting will further interest the potential buyer and make them get off the fence and into your Facebook Sales Funnel.

By increasing awareness in your product, extending the reach of your ads, engaging your potential and existing audience, your Facebook Ads will improve revenues and reduce costs.

Facebook Allows You to Find New Qualified Leads Easily by Including and Excluding

If your goal with Facebook Ads is to find new qualified leads to increase your customer base, Facebook can exclude your current clientele so that you can use your budget on acquiring new clients instead of clients that are already familiar with your business. For example, if your campaign is for newsletter subscriptions, you can exclude people that have already subscribed.

To exclude your current customers you must first create a Custom Audience from your existing list of customers. Then, while creating your ad, target a related interest or product and exclude the Custom Audience list that you just created.

To boost conversions by targeting potential customers that have visited your website, but left without converting, you can retarget them by using a Custom Audience from your website and simultaneously excluding those customers that have already converted.

To do this you must first create a Custom Audience from your website and include those people that purchased your product. Then, exclude people that completed a purchase and target only those people that added a product to their cart but did not make a purchase.

Chapter 12: First Phase of a Successful Facebook Campaign

Running a successful Facebook advertising campaign requires some initial planning before you go live since you will want to have important supporting elements in place beforehand.

Remember, preparing yourself ahead of time will improve the odds of having your Facebook campaign conclude successfully.

The first thing to do when planning a Facebook campaign is to identify what your business' main selling points are. Ask yourself what sets your products or services apart from those of your competitors. Look for ways that your offerings stand out from the rest of the field and plan on highlighting them. If you think you do something better than your competitors, prepare to state that in your Facebook campaign.

Next you will want to select imagery for your Facebook ad that suitably represents your product or service and is likely to be attractive to your target demographic. This will help increase your chances of attracting new leads, potential clients, shares and clicks.

When it comes to targeting your campaign, you will first need to determine where your target demographic is situated. If you run a local business with a physical location that can be visited, then you will probably want to target potential customers in your area. On the other hand, those who operate an Internet-based business may wish to advertise to a much broader group in terms of their geographic location. This may require testing to determine what gives the best results.

Another helpful planning process involves determining what special interests your target group may have so that you can tie your promotional efforts to those interests.

Ad Types and Budgeting

Once you have completed the planning phase described in the previous section, you are now ready to make specific decisions regarding choosing appropriate Facebook ad types and economic cost choices.

You will first want to choose a suitable ad type or types to use since Facebook provides businesses with several different options. Perhaps the most popular and cost-effective ads are marketplace ads. These include Facebook ads that have links to external websites, as well as sponsored stories, page post ads and Facebook objects. Each of these various Facebook ad types have their own benefits, so you will want to select the type or types that are best suited to your marketing objectives. For most business, a combination of add types will be optimal. You can then use the ad response results to determine which option is best for your particular business.

Next you will want to set an advertising budget to make sure that your costs do not exceed your anticipated benefits. Decide how much you want to spend each day on running your Facebook advertising campaign, and remember that you may need to spend some money on testing, at least initially, so that you can best appeal to your target market.

You can also select a bidding strategy that works best for your business. As you create an ad, you can choose what you will pay for a click, with higher payments typically resulting in more clicks. You will probably generally want to bid close to the maximum, but this can be something you test to assess what strategy gives optimal results.

Furthermore, Facebook gives you two cost models to select from. You can either choose the cost-per-click or CPC model or the cost-per-thousand-impressions or CPM model. A good plan could involve testing both to determine what gives the best results for your campaign.

Another important thing to consider will be whether you want your campaign to focus on conversion or engagement. Facebook defines a conversion as any action a person takes on your website. This may include things like checking out, registering for a newsletter, adding an item to their shopping cart, or viewing something. With respect to engagement, this term refers to the acts of liking, commenting or sharing a Facebook ad, page or post.

When it comes to generating sales, conversion may be your top priority, but for expanding the awareness of your brand, then engagement may be more relevant since a person taking these actions appears on their timeline, thereby potentially alerting their Facebook friends.

Landing Pages versus Lead Ads

Facebook allows you to promote your business by linking to a so-called landing page website, which is typically a single page marketing website designed to get a consumer to take some action, such as buy an eBook or fill out a form, for example. This requires the party to leave Facebook.

On the other hand, Facebook lead ads allow clients to sign up for something you are promoting or offering by using their email address without leaving Facebook.

Although you can and probably should test which of these promotional methods has the best results for your offerings and target audience, some preliminary research indicates that landing pages tend to have better results for desktop computer users, while lead ads tend to convert mobile users better.

Strong Offers

Facebook allows you to create offers that allow businesses to provide discounts to customers by posting an offer to a Facebook page. Offers can be used very effectively in a Facebook campaign to create engagement and generate potential business leads, so you will want to make them as strong as possible.

One of the advantages of using an offer for marketing is that offers are saved when people claim them, and this allows them to find the offer easily at a later time. People also get notifications to remind them about saved offers, and offers have a different appearance from other Facebook posts, so this makes them stand out.

You will generally also want to use the strongest commercially sound offer feasible to increase your chances of catching a possible client's attention, since getting their contact information can be essential to your future marketing campaigns. Facebook suggests that strong offers that involve at least 20% off or free merchandise tend to have the best chances of a favorable result.

Two basic types of offer can make sense for your business as follows:

- *Education, Train and Support* - These offer types typically provide a prospective client with useful information that might induce them to give you their contact information.

- *Give-away and Trial Offers* – These offer types can attract new potential clients by providing free gifts or product trials in exchange for their contact information.

Once again, it will probably make sense for your business to try both of these offer methods to see which works best, as well as to attract both sorts of people who respond best to each method.

Facebook offers are free of charge to businesses, and you can easily create one as follows:

THE ULTIMATE FACEBOOK LEAD MACHINE

(1) Navigate to the timeline of your business Facebook page.

(2) Just above your timeline, you will see a set of images with links below them. Click on the one that says "Create an Offer", and hit the Get Started button on the resulting informational page.

(3) Fill in the form with details about your offer and provide attractive imagery to go with it. In addition to giving your offer a title, description and expiration date, you can also attach up to five photos or one video to your offer, you can set up terms and conditions for your offer, and you can specify how many of each offer you wish to make available.

(4) Review the preview provided to make sure your offer reads appropriately and seems attractive.

(5) Click on the Create Offer button at the lower right of the form to transmit the offer to your page's timeline.

Note that you will be able to create several different types of offer. You can either provide a discount as a percentage off the normal price or as a certain amount off the normal price. You can also make a "buy one, get one free" type of offer, or you can simply give something away for free. Remember to make your offer as strong as possible by providing at least a 20% discount for best results.

Chapter 13: Second Phase of a Successful Facebook Campaign

Once you have set up a campaign on Facebook, you will then need to follow up on it by manage the resulting business leads it helps generate for you. This will involve the collection of potential client contact information and providing any suitable follow up.

To maintain a good business reputation, you will also need to respond quickly and appropriately to those interested in any offers you post on your timeline by keeping your word about providing the offered discount, service or item as advertised.

Lead Management

A lead is a business contact that has potential interest in your products or services. Ideally, all information about each business lead generated by your Facebook page should be entered into a database, spreadsheet or contact book for future marketing purposes. This process can also be automated if you or an expert you hire knows how to do so.

Lead information is generated whenever someone clicks on your Facebook Lead Ad. At this point, their Facebook contact information is automatically filled out on the online Lead Ad form. Users can then edit the form to enter additional contact details and any desired information you request.

Remember, this lead information is very valuable for your

business, so diligently collecting it in this manner will allow you to target additional offers and marketing efforts toward these leads, as well as to refer to their information at a later date for strategic marketing purposes such as determining which of your lead ad campaigns were the most successful and hence should be repeated.

Keep in mind that some countries have placed legal restrictions on the keeping of personal data, so review the relevant laws in your jurisdiction to help assure your compliance. As a general guideline, personal data obtained for any purpose should not be kept beyond its usefulness for that purpose and should be securely deleted thereafter. As a security precaution, you can also hold such information on an offline computer or in a secure electronic archive to help keep it safer from hacking attempts.

Some of the more important items you can hope to receive from each business lead generated by Facebook are the following:

- *Lead Source IDs* - This is an identification number that corresponds to the source that you obtained a new lead from. For example, the code number might refer to Facebook in general or to a specific Facebook group where an advertisement was posted. You can use this important lead source ID information to figure out which of your ads generated the most leads and hence may be worth using again in future. Note that setting up your lead information input forms to provide lead source IDs may require some knowledge of HTML.

- *Tags and Labels* - Ad tags — and more recently ad labels — allow you to organize Facebook ad campaigns, sets of ads, and ads. By tagging each of those items with an identifier or label, you can let users query ads by using numerous possible attributes.

- *Automated Follow Up* - To make your life easier, you can automate email responses to leads your Facebook ads generate. This may require some programming ability so is considered beyond the scope of this book.

Sales Automation

If you do not choose to automate your sales lead retrieval from Facebook, you would typically have to manually log into your Facebook Business Manager, choose to visit your Publishing Tools and export your leads in a CSV file. These leads will typically include first and last names and email addresses, among whatever other informational items you chose to collect for each lead.

You can then import those leads in CSV format into an interface that allows you to send out responsive emails to the leads. Taking this important step will help market your products or services. You can also provide the lead with an interesting offer, such as a significant discount coupon or a free ebook, for example.

Many people without the extra time to spare for following

this manual procedure will choose instead to automate their sales efforts after leads are generated by Facebook ads. If you do not have the expertise to program your own automated sales response interface, several vendors outside Facebook provide automated Facebook sales lead follow up services.

An example of an automated mailing service that interfaces easily with Facebook is MailChimp, which will also require you to pay for the premium Facebook app called Zapier that will add new Facebook leads generated by an ad campaign directly to your MailChimp distribution list. To use this service, you will first need to set up accounts at Facebook, MailChimp and Zapier, and then make a connecting Zap in Zapier that directs new leads to your MailChimp list. Note that this will only work with new leads. If you have old leads you wish to feed into MailChimp, then you will need to export a CSV file of those leads from Facebook and use the import function to include them in your MailChimp list.

Real Time Reporting

Facebook lead ads allow you to set up your leads to be instantly updated within your business' Customer Relationship Management or CRM system for further follow up.

The Graph Automated Programming Interface or API is a useful method for getting lead data into and out of Facebook. It consists of an HTTP-based API that can be used to retrieve new lead ads generated by your Facebook advertising efforts in real-time.

Webhooks are another option for real time lead reporting. It is especially helpful to integrate your CRM system with Facebook so that you can start to receive and retrieve leads in real time whenever a new lead is submitted via Facebook. At that point, you can be sent an update to notify you of the fact that a new lead has just become available. The information relevant to the lead can then be retrieved by accessing the API. Webhooks also let you query Facebook's Read API in order to retrieve the lead information once you have been notified that a new lead exists.

Facebook Ads Manager

This is a mobile app that lets you manage your Facebook ads while on the go. You can quickly create and track Facebook ads using your Android device with the app's efficient and useful tools. Creating ads can be done using photos and videos stored in your device's library. This allows you to rapidly reach people using ads on Facebook, as well as on Instagram and Audience Network.

Grow

Grow.com offers a useful service to help connect your data using its integrated set of apps, so that databases, CRMs, financials and spreadsheets can be coordinated and used to their best effect within your business. In essence, Grow assists you in bringing together and analyzing data spread across different sources into a customized interface from which you can obtain business insights in real-time to allow your enterprise to increase its growth rate based on factual marketing data as it arrives. You can set up your Grow dashboard in a few simple steps, and then choose the data you want to create a customized chart or compute various inbuilt metrics to analyze your business activity with. Grow also allows you to set a timer for refreshing your sales data so that you can keep it up to date. Customized Grow dashboards can also be constructed for each department, team or employee in your business, giving each group a set of data targeted to their specific needs.

Infusionsoft

This company provides an all-in-one sales and marketing Software as a Service or SaaS product on a subscription basis aimed at small businesses with less than 25 employees. Infusionsoft's integrated platform allows its clients to consolidate data regarding sales, marketing, leads, payments, customers, and more. Its services include making and hosting Web forms and links, executing automated campaigns, tracking ROI for campaigns, providing customer sales updates in real time, and managing databases. It also offers an e-commerce service that lets clients manage shopping carts, dynamic discounts, product pages, and coupon codes. The company also provides mobile apps that allows clients to manage their contacts.

Chapter 14: Top Five Facebook Marketing Mistakes

After reading this book, Facebook is probably going to become one of your best friends when it comes to marketing your products, services or brand.

You will therefore want to make sure that you follow Facebook's rules or you may risk having your business page taken down for a violation of Facebook's terms of service that it considers problematic.

In addition to avoiding policy violations, you will also want to keep from falling into several other common marketing traps. The sections below will describe these possible marketing mistakes in further detail.

Violating Facebook's Advertising Policy

Perhaps the worst marketing mistake you can make using Facebook is to violate their advertising policy. The first step to take to avoid doing this is to become familiar with what their policies are. When doing this, you will want to make sure that your product is not on their rather long list of prohibited content, and that it complies with any restrictions that may be applicable. In addition, there are certain types of information that Facebook Lead Ads cannot request and still remain in compliance.

Since Facebook's policies can change without notice, the best place to go to review a comprehensive summary of their advertising policies is at this link:

THE ULTIMATE FACEBOOK LEAD MACHINE

https://www.facebook.com/policies/ads/#

After reviewing that link, you will understand that Facebook has quite a few rules to follow, that only Facebook determines what breaks or doesn't break its rules, and that the difference is often not very clear. You will therefore want to do your best to assure that your ad complies with Facebook's current policies.

Another thing to keep in mind is that all Facebook ads are reviewed for compliance with the above advertising policy before they appear on Facebook. This review period is usually completed within a day, but it can take longer.

In general, the review process involves looking at an ad's images, its text, its targeting, its positioning, and the content appearing on the landing page the ad links to. Note that if the landing page is not functional, does not match what is being promoted in the ad, or does not comply with Facebook's advertising policies, then the ad may be rejected.

Once a person from Facebook has reviewed your ad and found it to be in compliance with its policies, you will get a notice informing you that your ad has been approved. At that point, Facebook will begin displaying your ad, with results then becoming available in the Ads Manager. If your ad was not approved, then you can elect to edit and resubmit it, appeal the decision, or cancel the ad.

Too Much Promotion, so Don't Be Pushy

While you may certainly and justifiably want to post about your accomplishments, one of the major mistakes a business can make is to annoy its audience by over promoting itself.

Your business page's Facebook followers will usually want to connect to your brand because they value it and like your products or services. Those are good things, but you do not want to overdo it and cross the fine line into over-promotional territory, or you may very well risk losing their support and hence the business you were trying to stimulate with your promotional efforts.

Also keep in mind that you can even overdo things that ordinarily might seem beneficial to your audience like discounts, freebies and other deals. Consider mixing those more promotional posts up with some inspiring human interest stories or satisfied customer testimonials relevant to your business.

Accordingly, remember to promote your brand by attempting to entertain, inspire and interact with your audience, since that is what the majority of Facebook users are looking for from the social media platform. You will therefore need to find interesting new ways to inspire those who visit your page and provide them with a good reason to connect to your business.

Don't Sell Too Little

Although this pitfall might seem rather obvious, if you fail to promote your business and sell your products or services with your posts and campaign lead ads, you may not achieve the marketing results you were hoping for with your Facebook business page.

As with many things in life, you will often get out of your Facebook business page what you put into it. Taking the time to promote your products and services to appropriate target audiences via Facebook is what will ultimately pay off for you by generating more leads that hopefully result in more business.

Ignoring or Not Responding to Posts and Comments

Potential or existing customers generally do not like to be ignored by a business, so do remember to keep that in mind when they make or respond to your posts on your business page to avoid making this all too common marketing mistake. Remember, they have invested their time and attention into engaging with your business page, so the very least you should do is acknowledge them with a polite reply.

One way to let your business page's Facebook audience know you care is to like and reply to their comments and questions in as positive, attentive and thoughtful a manner as possible. Always thank them for leaving a compliment, and make an effort to strengthen your public commitment to giving any client an excellent customer service experience.

Avoid insulting, demeaning or arguing with them in any way, and thank them for their honest — and hopefully favorable — feedback. Even if they were sharing an unpleasant experience, try your best to express sympathy and aim to make interacting with your business page on Facebook a much more positive experience for them, especially if your messages will be visible to the general public.

Chapter 15: How to Improve Your Facebook Ads

Making a strong marketing statement with your Facebook ads can make them well worth their rather modest price by getting you considerable interest for your business' products or services. This chapter is about how to make such a statement effectively by improving your Facebook ads to have greater appeal to your target audience.

To begin with, you will need to design your Facebook ad in a way designed to appeal to the demographic you are targeting. For example, your choice of color should resonate with the product and its target audience, while your language should reflect the nature of your brand authentically in a short and snappy manner. Images used should be remarkable and be designed to have a strong and favorable impact.

All of these things are preliminaries that you and/or your marketing team will want to consider before actually setting up a Facebook ad. Once you have decided on those key items, the next step will involve filling out the online form provided by Facebook to create and format a Facebook ad.

To get to that step, you can first navigate to Facebook's business page at this link:

https://www.facebook.com/business/

This portion of Facebook's website contains extensive information about marketing your business on Facebook, so be sure to browse around a bit to see if anything they offer looks good to you.

To start creating a Facebook ad, you can just click on the blue button in the upper right of the screen that says "Create an Ad" to get into the Ad Manager section of Facebook's website. If you have not yet created your Facebook business page, there is also an adjacent blue button that says "Create a Page" that allows you to do this and which you should click on first.

Before Facebook's Ad Manager interface will appear, you will first need to be logged into your business page's admin account to proceed. Just enter your Facebook login details, including email address and password. The website then processes some information before taking you to the Ad Manager interface. You will then see a series of menu items on the left hand side of the page that you can work through to tailor your ad campaign to your business needs and objectives.

The first decision you will want to make involves the objective of your Facebook campaign. Since this book is largely about business lead generation, that can be a good place for you to start by selecting the Lead Generation option under the Consideration column heading.

Once that is done, you will then need to set up an Ad Account. You will probably need to just select Create New to start the process of opening one up, and then fill in the required fields like Account Country, Currency and Time Zone.

Setting up the next section involves selecting Ad Set from the menu to the left side of the page. You can then choose a particular Facebook page to promote, as well as selecting your target Audience, your desired ad Placements, and your Budget and Schedule options.

Targeting Options

It is worth mentioning here the importance of selecting an appropriate audience for your ad that would best suit your business' products or services and your objective in creating the ad.

You can start this targeting process by selecting the Audience menu item to the left. You can then either hit the "Create New" tab to formulate a new audience or use an existing one you have previously saved by clicking on the "Use a Saved Audience" dropdown menu tab.

You can also target or exclude a custom audience based on a website they might have visited. In addition, you can select your ad's target audience based upon their location, age, gender and language.

Detailed targeting is also available that allows you to include or exclude people who match one of the listed demographics, interests or behaviors you specify. The interface offers a number of suggestions for this section that you can browse among to choose appropriate.

Formatting Your Ad

Next, you will want to format your ad by clicking on the Ad menu option to the left of the Ad Manager page. You will first have the opportunity to select among four formatting options for your ad that include Carousel, Single Image, Single Video and Slideshow.

The first following sections will cover each of the basic options for formatting your Facebook ad, along with some ideal strategies for choosing among those available.

Images and Videos

Now you are ready to add some images and text to your ad. You can select a compelling image for your ad from among your Library photos or free stock images, as well as being able to upload some additional images or even use a video.

The recommended size for lead ad images to make sure your image always has a high quality look is 1200 x 628 pixels with a 1.9 to 1 image ratio. For videos, the ideal aspect ratio is 16:9 or 1:1 and the .mp4 format is best. Other preferred video specifications include: H.264 video compression, high profile, square pixels, a fixed frame rate, and progressive scan.

Remember to avoid having too much text on your ad image since that may result in an increased cost and a notably diminished reach for your ad due to Facebook's strong preference for a text-free ad image.

Basically, no more than 20 percent of the image area should be text, and this includes all image slides within a carousel of images. Note that things like logos, watermarks and numbers will also count as text if they are incorporated into your ad image.

Headline

The Headline of your ad will be the text that displays prominently in a large font below your ad image. Facebook recommends that you keep ad Headlines to no more than 25 characters in order for them to be displayed well on smaller screens. This text should be attention-grabbing, short and punchy.

Body Copy

The Body Copy of your ad appears in a smaller size font just above the ad image and will consist of the text you use to provide a greater depth of information to potential clients about your product or service being advertised. For optimal display purposes, Facebook recommends that you keep your Body Copy to a maximum of 90 characters.

Link Description

The Link Description should be limited to 30 characters for best display results. It will appear in a smaller font below the ad's Headline on your Facebook News Feed.

Call to Action

The Call to Action or CTA is a button that you can include in your Facebook ads to promote some activity you wish business leads or potential clients to perform.

Various types of CTA actions are supported by Facebook, and these include: Apply Now, Download, Get Quote, Learn More, Sign Up and Subscribe. You will want to select the CTA button option that seems most appropriate for your business needs.

Lead Form

You can create a Lead Form to use in your Facebook ads that will allow people to send you their contact information. Using this option is a great idea for most business promotions looking to expand the number of potential new client leads.

In order to set up a new Lead Form, just click on the icon shown and it will take you to a new menu where you can enter a name for the form at the top. Below that, you can change your form's Welcome Screen headline, image, layout and button.

You can then edit its Questions that inquire about information you wish to collect; your Privacy Policy that details how you intend to use or share this collected information; and the Thank You Screen that will be shown after the Lead Form has been submitted and which can also contain a link to your website.

Settings

You can also click on Settings at the top of the Lead Form box to choose a form language from a drop down menu and allow the retrieval of organic leads by checking the appropriate box.

In addition, you can edit the Form Configuration, which includes the Field IDs that are collected on the form and which are initially set to Email and Full Name by default.

Reviewing and Placing Your Ad Order

Once all of the above information has been entered for your ad, you can click on the Review Order button on the lower right of the page to see a summary of the information you entered.

You will then be given an opportunity to fix any errors that Facebook picks up. Once that has been done, you can click on the Place Order button to send your ad order to Facebook for their final approval and implementation.

Chapter 16: Types of Facebook Ads

Different types of Facebook ads and marketing strategies can be used to further the various advertising objectives your business has. It first makes sense to think about and write down exactly what those objectives are.

You can do this in a specific Facebook marketing plan, or you can even include them as part of an overall business plan you create for your enterprise to focus its efforts and/or attract new investors.

The following sections discuss a variety of possible business objectives you can further with Facebook Ads, as well as what type of ad or ads probably make the most sense for you to use.

Boost Your Post

The first type of Facebook ad to be covered here is that designed to boost a post you have made to your Facebook business page.

For example, a Facebook post to your business page can be about the benefits of a product or service your business provides; about a sale you are planning to hold to attract new business; or regarding a discount offering intended to reward existing customers and encourage repeat business from them.

To boost your post is a fairly inexpensive and cost-effective method to get your business page content in front of more people. The process of boosting a post is relatively simple and straightforward — and it can be done right from your Facebook business page — so do not hesitate to use this important method for increasing exposure for your business when it makes economic sense to do so. You can also set your budget for this key type of post promotion to any amount you can afford and wish to pay.

Boosting a post means more existing and potential clients will see it, including those you can target, and it has been shown to be a useful means to promote special events you are hosting and to disseminate news about your products and services.

The process of post boosting starts with the following steps:

(1) Navigate to the post you would like to boost. It can either be a new one or one that you already posted to your business page's timeline.

(2) Click on the "Boost Post" button situated at the lower right of the post box.

Once you do that, a Facebook ad will be immediately generated from your original post.

You will then need to select an audience to promote your boosted post to. One option you have at this point is to choose groups of people to target your post boost to by specifying who you wish to show your post to. This process includes selecting you target audience's physical locations, age, genders and personal interests based on what appears on their Facebook profiles.

Another option you have is to promote your post to those people who have already liked your Facebook business page and their friends. Note that you can only use this very useful option if over fifty people have already liked your page.

The next step when boosting a post involves choosing an appropriate budget for this advertising activity. You can do this by setting a maximum budget, and you can elect to spend more or less as your business purpose requires. For each chosen budget, Facebook will provide you with an estimated amount of people you can expect to reach for that amount of money.

Once that budget setting process has been completed, you will need to choose the duration or time period in which your post boost is to remain active. Although your post will be boosted for a single day by default, you can choose to boost it for up to a week.

When all of the above steps have been finalized to your satisfaction, just click on the "Boost" button to finish this post boosting process and start enjoying the numerous benefits.

Promote Your Page

Promoting your business page on Facebook is typically done by creating an ad for your page that will be shown on both desktop and mobile Facebook platforms. You can do this by following this procedure:

(1) Click on the "Promote Your Page" button situated under the profile picture on your Facebook page.
(2) When a pop up window appears, select your target audience, the budget you have to spend per day, and the time frame or duration that you wish to promote your page for.
(3) Click on the "Promote Page" button.

In addition to using the default options, you can select among some additional options for promoting your page. To do this, simply click in the lower corner of the pop up window to the left and choose "Advanced Options".

Facebook also lets you test the effects of its other ad options right from your business page. These include promoting your local business or your website, as well as creating a custom ad to get more targeting and creative options.

Reach People Near You

Many local businesses who have a Facebook page and wish to use it for marketing their goods or services will want to reach out to people who live nearby or whose devices indicate they are visiting that area and hence might become customers.

A big advantage of Facebook is that it allows you to readily reach people situated in the cities, communities and countries where your business is situated or wishes to focus at least a portion of its advertising budget on.

For example, a local restaurant can choose to show Facebook ads to people whose profiles indicate they are living in the same community that the venue operates in or in nearby surrounding areas.

You can easily do this by selecting a target audience and specifying their location when you set up a Facebook ad. For example, you can target your audience by:

- Country
- State
- Province
- City
- Congressional districts
- ZIP or postal codes
- Worldwide
- Free Trade Areas
- Continents or Regions
- Markets

You can even drop a pin on a map provided by Facebook and aim your advertising at people inside a certain specified radius of that pin.

Increase Brand Awareness

Boosting the public's or a target audience's awareness of your business' brands is something that Facebook ads can be very useful for. You can elect to connect and share information about your business with your core audience, a custom audience or even lookalike audiences that may have similar interests.

Increasing brand awareness will typically be done with Facebook ads that use photos, videos, slideshows, carousels, links or canvases. By reaching out to show people on Facebook things they are most interested in, you can motivate them to engage with your business and discover more about your brands.

In terms of controlling where your Facebook ad is shown, the platform lets a business widen its reach by selecting multiple locations where Facebook users will get to view its ad. Connecting with Instagram is another option for increasing brand awareness.

After all of your Facebook marketing efforts have been put into motion, you then also have the ability to monitor their success rates to see if they have achieved your desired advertising objectives. Most people will use the Ads Manager Facebook provides to do this important analysis. Audience Insights is another useful Facebook service business managers can use to help them understand their enterprises' target audience better.

Send People to Your Website

Facebook is great for keeping your business' contacts and clients up to date on your latest events, discounts and product or service offerings. Nevertheless, Facebook can also act as a useful conduit to get existing or potential clients to visit your official website where more permanent information about your company can be displayed.

THE ULTIMATE FACEBOOK LEAD MACHINE

Facebook can also easily direct people to your business' blog page or site. Blogs are helpful when you want to display longer articles that might go further into depth on subjects than is common on Facebook. Ideally, the blog will also deal with topics of particular interest to those who may patronize your business.

One way to start this process of funneling people to your website or blog page from Facebook is to go to Facebook's Ad Manager and click on the "Create an Advert" option. You will then be shown a selection of options. Choose the 'Send people to your website' option, and put in your website's full web address or URL.

In most cases, this address will probably direct clients to your official website's home page or a product sale landing page, although you can also direct interested parties to a web page where a form is situated that asks a potential client to enter an email address, some personal details and perhaps even a brief message so that you can capture a potential business lead.

Another option for promoting your website is available using the Boost option situated in the menu to the left of your Facebook page. After you click on that, you will be taken to a page where you can select "Get More Website Visitors". Just click on that to be taken to a page where you can set up a Facebook ad optimized for that result.

A third option involves adding the "Learn More" button to the lower right corner of the cover image situated at the top of your Facebook business page. This important button can be set up to take interested parties who click on it directly to a website of your choice. You will need to enter the correct link to make that work. You can also test the link, and can change the link as desired by placing your mouse's cursor over the button and choosing the "edit button" option from the resulting pull down menu. This same menu even lets you view an Insights page that gives you information about how many website clicks that button has achieved over the past week.

Get Installs and Engagement for Your App

If you have written an application or app that can be advertised via Facebook, then you can use Facebook's Ad Manager to encourage users to obtain, install and interact with your app.

You can enter the Ad Manager interface by clicking on the pull down menu to the right of the question mark situated in the upper right hand side of the blue bar on the top of a Facebook page. The item to click on with your mouse looks like a downwards pointing arrow. You can then select the Create Ads option.

You will then see a loading screen that says the interface is preparing your new ad account, connecting to your pages and getting things ready for you to create a Facebook ad. Once this process completes, you will be left in Facebook's Ad Manager that has a grey bar on the top of the page to distinguish it from most Facebook pages.

Now that you are in Ad Manager, the first thing you will need to clarify is your marketing objective. Under the column entitled "Consideration", choose the "App Installs" option by clicking on it. This will send people to the app store so that they can buy your app. At that point, you will just complete the ad creation process by going through the subsequent menus.

Raise Attendance for Your Event

Any public event can be promoted on Facebook in order to raise awareness and attendance for it. You will first need to associate your event with your business Facebook page so that your event ad will be included in Facebook's news feed. When you create public events on your personal profile's timeline, they will only show up as ads in Facebook's right side column.

To promote an event, you first need to set one up, which is a free service Facebook provides. You do this by navigating to your Facebook business page and clicking on the "..." situated just below your cover image and immediately to the right of the Share button. A drop down menu will appear that includes a Create Event option.

After selecting that, you will be shown a new event creation form that you will need to fill in with basic details about the event, including a description, date, start and end times, and location. You can also include a promotional image designed to draw attention to the event. You can list the names of co-hosts, relevant keyword sets, and a ticket sale URL address. Additional features include being able to designate who can post and to display a guest list of people who indicate they plan on attending or who have purchased tickets. Once you have entered all of those details and confirmed your intention to post the event, you event's post will appear on your business page's timeline and can also show up in the news feed.

Now that you have a Facebook page and an event to advertise already set up, you can start promoting your event on Facebook's news feed. To promote your event, you can follow these simple steps:

(1) Navigate to your event and click on "Promote Event".
(2) When the event promotion form appears, just fill in all the relevant details pertaining to your event ad, which will include its target audience and the advertising budget you are willing to spend.
(3) Once the form is completed, you can just click on "Place Order" to finish the process.

Get Video Views

Videos may take more time to create than text or an image, but they have become a great way to market your business on Facebook. In part, this is because videos tend to get more attention and Facebook news feed exposure than either text posts or photos.

Some of the primary ways to enhance the number of views you get for a promotional video can include using one or more of the following strategies:

(1) Be inspiring to your audience.
(2) Offer educational material directed at your audience's interests.
(3) Entertain your audience.

Facebook has also been in the process of rolling out a featured video service where a chosen video can now be highlighted on your timeline. It will also appear above your page's About section and will be larger when seen from the Videos tab so that it stands out to viewers.

You can also include a Call to Action (CTA) button on your cover image that sends people who click on it to a video address that you have chosen to link to it.

Collect Leads for Your Business

Perhaps one of the best ways to generate and collect leads for your business using Facebook is to employ Lead Ads. This very useful form of Facebook ad lets other users show their interest in either a product or a service you are offering by filling a form out with their contact details and other useful information. You can even include customized questions tailored to your business' information needs.

It is quite easy to download leads directly from Facebook to manage them yourself. Alternatively, your leads can be connected to a Customer Relationship Management or CRM system like MailChimp or Salesforce. Such tools help companies track, report on and maintain their relationships with clients, including other firms and individual customers.

As examples of Lead Ad usage, some businesses might employ Lead Ads to collect newsletter sign ups or to obtain requests for price quotes. Others might use the leads generated by Facebook to take a more personal customer approach by having their Lead Ads acquire contact information for a subsequent follow up sales call or perhaps for disseminating business information to potential clients.

The information gathering forms used in Lead Ads are created and can be modified as part of the Lead Ad process that Facebook takes you through. These forms can even be set up to take essential information from the user's Facebook profile automatically instead of the user having to type in that information manually. Such populated forms allow users to edit and then confirm their information by clicking on the "Submit" button to send it.

In addition to collecting useful information, the responses these Lead Ads generate will usually allow a business to follow up on each generated lead by having a sales staff member contact the interested party.

Before you actually try to set up a Lead Ad, you will first want to prepare the information you intend to ask potential leads for and any images or videos you intend to include in your ad. You will also need to provide a URL that links to a privacy policy statement that your business displays on its official website, which is required by Facebook for all Lead Ads.

Another useful feature of Lead Ads is that you can create a Welcome Screen that allows you to provide more information about your business activities along with your ad.

Anyway, now that you know why Facebook Lead Ads are so useful and have collected all necessary information to set one up, you will need to follow these steps to do so:

(1) On your Facebook business page, click on the "…" to the right of the "Share" button located just below your cover photo and select "Ads Manager" from the drop down menu. Choose the appropriate ad account from the list shown, if any.
(2) When viewing Campaign Objective, select "Lead generation" — which is situated below the "Consideration" column — by clicking on it.
(3) Click on "Page", which is located under "Ad Set" in the menu at the left side of the page to choose the Facebook page you want to use to generate leads for by selecting it from a pull down menu.
(4) Accept Facebook's Lead Ads Terms for that page.
(5) You can then select an Audience, Placements, Budget and Schedule for your Lead Ad.
(6) Click on "Format", which is located under "Ad" in the menu at the left side of the page to choose how you want your Lead Ad to look, including any images or videos you wish to incorporate. You can also Edit the text of the ad under this heading, as well as modify the customizable Lead Form that Facebook shows to potential business leads for them to fill in.
(7) You can then either click the Review Order button to look over your Lead Ad details or the Place Order button to confirm them. Both buttons are located at the lower right of the screen.

This step by step guide will get you through the basic Lead Ad setup process, but do note that a number of Advanced Options exist for many of the above steps that you should check out just in case they might be helpful for your business.

Increase Conversions on Your Web Site

Facebook ads can be optimized to get people to act in specific desirable ways on your website, and when they do this, it is known as a website conversion.

Examples of constructive website actions you might wish to promote via Facebook may include: signing up for a newsletter, paying for a product, making an appointment for a service, registering for a webinar, filling out a lead form, or downloading a report or ebook.

To do this within Facebook's Ad Manager, you select Conversions under the Conversion column under the Campaign Objective menu choice, and then click on the Website or Messenger radio button. At this point, you need to create and install a Facebook Pixel on your website, which is a piece of JavaScript code placed on a website to improve Facebook ad performance by measuring, optimizing and building audiences.

You will then need to proceed to fill out the other details of your ad, including its Offer, Audience, Placements, Budget, Schedule, Ad Format, Ad Page and Ad Links.

If you have any questions about how each of these ad elements work and what they are used for, Facebook's Ad Manager usually includes a "Learn More" link beside each one.

Get People to Claim Your Offer

You can create an offer for a product that has a discounted price, a coupon or another special deal you are interested in offering to existing or prospective clients.

Note that you cannot delete such offers once they are created, so be sure you have set them up correctly and are prepared to follow through on what you are offering.

Offers become posts to your timeline that are saved when people claim them so that they can find them again. In addition, people get notifications about offers they have saved, and offers have a different appearance from other posts so they tend to stand out on your page's timeline.

You can start the process of creating an offer directly from your Facebook business page. Just click the "Create an offer" icon situated near the top of your page's timeline under its Cover Photo.

It may be helpful for you to select a targeted audience for the offer ad you are planning on running that best suits your marketing objective. You can even decide how many people can claim or take advantage of your offer before it is withdrawn, as well as setting how long your offer will run for.

Within the Create an Offer dialog, you get to select where the offer is available, its relevant URL, the offer title and description. You can also add up to five images, and enter the date when the Offer expires. Just click on the blue Create Offer button at the lower left of the dialog box to finalize your Offer.

Promote a Product Catalog

A Product Catalog consists of the information about all of the product items you want to advertise using your Facebook ads. Subsets of related product items are known as Product Sets, while the file that a product catalog holds that contains information about each product is known as a Product Feed.

Every line within the Product Catalog's Product Feed file has a product description that includes an ID, a name, a category, its availability, the product URL, the image URL and other relevant product attributes.

Product Catalogs can be used with several types of Facebook ads and formats, including dynamic and collection ads. You can also mark a product out of stock or automatically update the availability of products.

The major advantage of using Product Catalogs with dynamic Facebook ads is that you can target clients who look over your catalog without purchasing anything. Your Facebook pixel will track the website pages your customer browsed and then automatically display a relevant ad to them to induce them to buy.

If you want to promote relevant products from your catalog to interested customers, you can select the Facebook advertising objective of "Product Catalog Sales" under the Conversion column displayed in Ad Manager under the Campaign Objective menu option. You will also need to create a Product Catalog, a Pixel and a dynamic ad to finish the process.

Chapter 17: How to Build a Facebook Ad

Facebook ads are an excellent tool in a marketing arsenal that can be used to promote just about any business, product or service to existing or potential clients that have Facebook accounts.

This chapter will first show some samples of various types of Facebook ads so you will get a sense of what to expect. It will also cover the key elements of Facebook ads and give you pointers on how to put them all together to build a suitable Facebook ad for your business.

Also keep in mind that Facebook ads may also have different appearances when viewed in the right column or on a mobile or desktop device. You can review what your ad will look like by using the "Ad Preview and Placement" section in the tool you use to create ads with. This will let you preview your ad as you are setting it up and thereby make sure it looks good in all possible placement situations.

Overall, you will probably want to aim for a short catchy headline, a brief explanation, an appropriate and eye-grabbing image and a link for further details in most of your Facebook ads.

Samples of Various Types of Ads

The first thing to decide upon when building your Facebook ad is what type of ad imagery to use, and you will usually want to make sure to include an interesting graphical approach.

Although taking a creative approach to graphics is probably best since novelty is so attractive, if that seems beyond your abilities or budget, you can simply choose to use an ad with an appropriate image.

Other visual ad options include attaching a video or even displaying a carousel that is made up of multiple images, which are typically interesting and related, and are displayed in a looped sequence.

Remember that your ad's imagery will be the thing most likely to capture the attention of your audience, so do not skimp on this part of your Facebook advertising campaign. Also, if you will be posting your ad to your business page's timeline, then remember that posts with videos tend to be more likely to hit the news feed of your page's followers.

The following three sections will provide examples and describe these imagery options in greater detail so you can decide for yourself which makes the most sense for you to use in your Facebook ad.

Creative Imagery

It usually helps if you can come up with something especially creative for your ad's graphics, since that tends to get more attention from viewers.

Many Facebook users are a bit jaded from already seeing so many ads, so having something visual that stands out can really increase your ad's success rate in terms of attracting clicks.

Ad with Image

Perhaps the simplest, and yet very effective, type of Facebook ad graphics involves including just a single image with your ad. The more enigmatic or mysterious your image, while still appearing relevant to their interests, the more likely your ad is to get clicked on by a viewer.

Another good idea when using a single image in your Facebook ads is to test several different ones to determine which you get the best response to. At least two or three image variations would probably make sense initially. This should help you improve the performance of your Facebook ad campaign significantly.

Furthermore, it is very important to remember here that Facebook ad images should probably not have more than twenty percent of their area consisting of text. Facebook currently allows more than that, but you do stand the risk that your ad's reach will be diminished or even eliminated if you put more text inside your ad's image.

Since this image text policy can change, it makes sense to check with Facebook first to find out how much image text is presently advisable when you go to create your ad image if you intend to include any text at all in the image.

Ad with a Video

Facebook ads with videos tend to get more exposure on page follower news feeds than those with just an image or text.

Creating a more complex video relevant to your business purposes for the ad can often take a bit of a production budget. You may need to pay a videographer for the filming, although you can take video footage yourself with a smartphone. In addition, you will either need to pay a video editor or learn how to use a video editing program to do scene editing, as well as add titles, a soundtrack and perhaps also some still imagery.

Nevertheless, some low budget Facebook ads just use a quick and easy screen capture video containing one or two still images, since a video is a video when it comes to getting preferential treatment on Facebook's news feed.

Ad with Multiple Images in a Carousel

If you really think you need several images to convey what your Facebook ad is about to viewers, you can use a carousel.

The carousel format lets you highlight as many as ten images or videos inside a single Facebook ad. Each of these items is known as a card, and each card can even have its own unique link.

Using a carousel can help you increase the amount of creative space an ad has. You can also focus on different products or services, as well as on various details related to a single product or service. You can even offer various promotions.

Some businesses have found it useful to employ carousels to tell a story related to their brand that evolves over each card contained in the carousel. Just about any business can use this helpful and popular ad format to achieve various advertising goals, so it makes sense to at least see if it might be suitable for you.

In general, it makes sense to at least consider using a carousel if you wish to direct your ad's viewers to more than one link.

Text

The next important thing to focus on will be writing the text for your ad. Unless you are advertising an informative article or blog post, for which some introductory text and a link might be suitable, you will probably want to put together some ad text that is very catchy to grab the attention of your audience quickly and hold it to the point where they can be directed toward providing the response you want.

Also remember to use as brief a number and as simple a selection of words as possible so that they can be readily understood by the broadest cross-section of people, many of whom might have a limited attention span.   Keep your text short and concise. Most experts recommend you use 90 characters or fewer, if at all possible, in your ad text.

Furthermore, avoid writing extraneous text, and keep your ad's written words tightly focused on the purpose of your ad and in directing its viewers toward what you are trying to

achieve by running it.

Other helpful things to include in your ad text to increase lead generation and activity in response to your ad might include:

- Discounts that provide responding potential clients with a reduced price on products or services offered by your business,
- Offers of free promotional items if the person responds to your ad,
- Questions you can ask of potential or existing clients to get them to interact with your ad by clicking on it, and
- Product feedback requests that can give you useful information about your products or services and show potential clients that you care about their opinions.

Another good idea is to include something in your ad text known as a "time prompt" when it seems suitable. For example, you can employ special time sensitive text — such as "Now", "Today" and "Limited Time Only" — in order to stress upon potential and existing clients the importance of them taking prompt action on whatever you happen to be promoting with your ad.

Headline

Each ad will have a headline that can be up to 25 characters in length. This is limited space, so your ad headlines must be as punchy, short and attention grabbing as possible to be effective and at the same time remain within the tight amount of available headline space. You will also want your headline to create an explanatory context for the imagery you choose to display with your ad.

One popular strategy is to make your Facebook ad headlines very attractive, yet vague enough to get those who see your ad to click on them.

Depending on the ad topic they are trying to write for, many ad designers might use catchy questions like: "Ready to make thousands from home?" or "Want a virtual friend?"

Simplicity is a virtue in headlines, and both of these simple questions have an implied "you" in them that talks straight to the reader. They also tend to induce curiosity clicks just so the reader can find out more about what you are offering.

Furthermore, to keep things interesting for your audience, remember to use action verbs in your headline that can often start a sentence. Examples might be:

- Ready
- Want
- Play
- Try
- Fight
- Love
- Avoid

Another headline writing tip is to cut out unnecessary words. As an example of this, you could theoretically write something fairly long for a title like: "Do You Love Riding

Horses?" A more succinct version would be: "Love Riding Horses?", while just a super brief two-word question might suffice, like: "Love Riding?" perhaps.

Furthermore, putting an air of attractive mystery into your ad headline can often spark curiosity in a reader that leads to those all-important ad clicks. Nevertheless, you will want to aim for being enigmatic instead of vague so that a person in your target audience can readily decide whether or not they are interested enough in what you have to offer to bother to click on your ad.

The final thing to remember about headlines is that all of the smart text you carefully craft will probably not make a totally disinterested person respond to your ad. As a result, you will want to focus on writing a headline that appeals to those people who are most likely to be potential leads for your business and who you are targeting with the particular ad you are writing.

News Feed Link Description

Facebook offers two types of ads: those that appear to the right of the Facebook page — which many viewers tend to ignore — and those ads that appear directly in a user's news feed.

You will need to have already set up a Facebook page for your business in order to purchase a news feed ad. In general, news feed ads tend to be more visible to readers since they often scan through their Facebook news feed for information about their friends and family members, as well as posts from groups they have joined and pages they are following.

News Feed ads therefore tend to generate more qualified new business leads, that is provided you are able to do some effective audience targeting for your product, service or promotion anyway.

The News Feed Link Description appears immediate below the headline in any news feed ad in a smaller font. When it comes to choosing what to enter in the Newsfeed Link Description field, you will want to inform people about why it would be a great idea for them to visit your business or take other action you are promoting with you ad.

In addition, you will need to be brief, especially since your News Feed Link Description should not run more than about 200 characters in length. Also make sure to give customers a sense of where they are going to be transferred to by clicking on the link and what to expect when they choose to do so.

Finally, since this ad description will show up in the news feed of Facebook users, do remember to target this brief piece of text at people looking at their news feed and to make it as attention grabbing as possible within the space available.

Display URL

Remember that the web address or Display URL you decide to link to your ad will want to be chosen to make it easy for clients to do what you want them to do with this ad. Accordingly, consider linking your ad directly to a particular web page that features a specific action or actions you want customers to perform, instead of just linking the ad to your website's welcome page.

As part of your test marketing, you can also create several different ads with alternative Display URLs and styles to see which ad version has the best results when it comes to meeting your marketing objectives.

Call to Action

A Call to Action or CTA involves signaling the customer that some sort of activity on their part is being suggested to them. Facebook ads generally include a call to action button with a simple command displayed in text format and which tells them exactly what you wish them to do.

The currently available examples of acceptable CTA button text include the following words or brief phrases:

- Shop Now
- Learn More
- Sign Up
- Book Now
- Download

It makes sense to include a valid and relevant Call to Action button in your Facebook ad because it can really help send more traffic to your website or direct potential clients to take another desirable action that will benefit your business purposes.

THE ULTIMATE FACEBOOK LEAD MACHINE

Tracking

Although the practice is admittedly somewhat controversial among those who value privacy on the Internet, visitors to any website that has a Facebook "Like" or "Share" button on it are currently being tracked by Facebook.

What this tracking means to an advertiser is that information about people browsing such pages online and their interests is being collected and used by Facebook and its algorithms to display targeted ads within Facebook and to keep users looking at and interacting with their site for longer times.

While Windows and Android users are still largely unable to block such tracking from taking place, Apple's iOS 9 has a "Content Blockers" feature that now allows users to install third party apps that block content shown in the Safari web browser. This lets them also block social media widgets like Facebook's "Like" and "Share" buttons.

Pixel Tracking

The Facebook Pixel has already been introduced, and this very useful feature lets you track key actions that your business leads perform, including registering for things and making purchases.

It makes especially good sense for businesses to include the Facebook pixel on their website in the following situations:

(1) *You want to track conversions* – Installing the

Facebook pixel lets Facebook report back to you about the number of actions your Facebook ads have resulted in.

(2) *You want to optimize conversions* – the Facebook pixel lets Facebook learn which people who view you ads seem more likely to perform a certain action on your website. You can use this information to optimize your ad delivery to yield more of these desirable actions.

(3) *You want to build custom audiences* – You can actually record all page visits and actions from every visitor to your website, and not just visitors that happen to click on Facebook ads to get there. This data can be used to formulate Website Custom Audiences you can use for retargeting purposes when using Facebook Ads.

The Facebook pixel provides you with a list of standard events that can be used with your website. Such events can be employed for Custom Audiences and conversions, as well as for conversion tracking and optimization purposes.

In addition, the Facebook pixel will let you use custom events that can be used along with either Custom Audiences or custom conversions.

The following chapter will describe in greater detail how results obtained from pixel tracking can be used in developing re-targeting and re-marketing strategies for Facebook ads.

Chapter 18: Facebook Re-targeting and Re-marketing

When people have already come in contact with your brand online via Facebook or a site that uses your Facebook pixel, you have the option of approaching them again. This is often a very worthwhile approach for businesses to take when it comes to generating fresh sales. There exist two main ways to make this fresh approach and these are known on Facebook as re-marketing and re-targeting.

Re-marketing usually involves re-engaging customers in other medium, often using an email campaign. This method of brand promotion is often used on clients who have abandoned their shopping carts. It can also be used to up or cross sell similar items to those someone already purchased. Lifecycle marketing emails are another re-marketing option.

On the other hand, re-targeting usually refers to online ad placements, as well as display ads, that are shown based upon the activity a user performs while on your website. This information can be obtained from cookies or Facebook pixels, and once you have it, you can target ads to them when they visit other sites. This process takes place via networks like AdBrite and the Google display network, which can reach users on millions of websites other than your own.

This chapter will focus on how to implement these approaches via Facebook using Tracking Pixels, as well as Custom and Lookalike Audiences.

Tracking Pixels

As has already been mentioned, tracking pixels are a great way for advertisers to optimize for and keep track of certain specific actions. Conversion tracking focuses on actions leading to offsite conversions or to externally hosted Facebook tabs.

For example, the conversions that can be tracked via tracking pixels include the following:

- Registration
- Checkouts
- Add to Cart
- Key Page Views
- Leads
- Other website conversions

If you using a tracking pixel on the website to which your ads are directed, Facebook can track each of these offsite conversions to help you calculate the return on your investment in Facebook ads.

The Facebook pixel consists of a few rather simple lines of JavaScript that you can just copy from Facebook's website and then paste into the source code for each page of your own website. Once installed, you can verify that your Facebook pixel works by getting FB Pixel Helper installed on the toolbar of your Internet browser.

Once you have added the Facebook pixel to your website, the next step will be associating it with a Facebook Ad so that you can start using it for tracking purposes. Various events can then be tracked, and you can also use the pixel with other Facebook marketing products like Dynamic Product Ads, Website Custom Audiences and Conversion Tracking.

These products let you use desirable actions that have been tracked to retarget your audiences for marketing purposes, obtain new clients and even track Facebook ad conversions. You can also let Facebook automatically optimize your ads on the platform to produce more of these desirable actions.

Custom Audiences

One of the best things about Facebook that any business can take advantage of with a bit of effort is that you can create a Custom Audience on Facebook to target advertising to.

For example, you can use an existing customer list you may have lying around to generate a Custom Audience. This could a general list, it could be based on specific interests those clients have or it could be focused on their purchase history. You can then use Facebook to target ads specifically to the audience you've created. This same audience can not only be targeted on Facebook, but also on Instagram.

Custom Audiences can also be used with promotions using the Audience Network where ads are published outside Facebook, thereby extending your marketing reach to new places.

Audience Network allows you extend ad campaigns beyond Facebook to promote to selected audiences via mobile apps, websites and videos. The targeting, measurement and delivery used is the same as Facebook to ensure that each Audience Network ad gives you an opportunity to attain your ad campaign objectives at a reasonable price. Audience Network comes up as a placement choice for ads when you select one of these objectives for it:

- Traffic
- Conversions
- App Installs
- Engagement
- Product catalog sales
- Video Views.

Facebook reviews the publishers involved with Audience Network to ensure their content, websites and apps conform to Facebook's standards. You will either need to copy and paste or upload your customer list, and then data from it will be used by Facebook to match people on your list with people already on Facebook.

Once you have a customer file created, you are ready to begin the process of creating a Custom Audience. To begin this process, follow this procedure:

(1) Go to your Facebook Audiences.
(2) If you already have at least one audience, you can just click on the "Create Audience" pull down menu and choose the "Custom Audience" option. If you do

not, then click on "Create a Custom Audience".
(3) Click on: "Customer File".
(4) Click on: "Add from your own file".

You then have several additional steps to take in order to create your Custom Audience. They are as follows:

Add Customer File:

Do this either by uploading a file in text or CSV format, or by copying and pasting it in the "Paste your content here" blank. Give your new Custom Audience a name and description. Facebook even offers a template data file you can use to get started.

Edit Data Mapping:

Facebook will display a preview of your data and how they would classify it into one of three possible status categories. A lot of errors might signal Facebook is looking for the wrong delimiter between data points. This can be changed by hovering above "modify the delimiter" and selecting another. Your previewed data can also have its type and format changed, and you can remove data from match consideration. When satisfied, click "Create & Upload".

Hashed Upload and Creation:

Facebook will automatically hash your data, upload it and create an audience for you. This can take some time for large files, so you can just set it going in a background tab of your browser while you do something else.

Next Steps:

Once your Custom Audience has been created, Facebook will automatically show the most effective next steps they recommend for you to proceed to. You can either choose to take one of those steps right away, or you click on "Done" to complete this process.

Lookalike Audiences

Among the Next Steps you can choose from after you have created a Custom Audience is the option to put together a Lookalike Audience. You must have created that Custom Audience to make a Lookalike Audience from it. Also, only a page or pixel admin can opt to create a Facebook Lookalike Audience, and those using mobile app install data will need to be either an admin or a developer for that app.

Make sure you have the appropriate authority before attempting to proceed to create a Lookalike Audience. Here is the procedure to follow:

(1) Navigate to your Audiences
(2) Click on the "Create Audience" dropdown menu and select the "Lookalike Audience" option from it.
(3) Select your data source, which can be:
    a. a Custom Audience you created,
    b. data from your Facebook pixel,

    c. your mobile app's data, or

    d. those who have liked your Facebook page.

(4) Select the country or countries that you expect you may find a similar group of people in.

(5) Select the size of your desired audience using the slider. This cannot later be edited without creating a new Lookalike Audience.

(6) Click on the "Create Audience" button.

Note that you can also create a Lookalike Audience when you are involved in the ad creation process in either Ads Manager or Power Editor.

Another important thing to keep in mind is that Lookalike Audiences may take up to 24 hours to create. The audience will also refresh after three to seven days while you continue using it to target ads to. You can check the last time your Lookalike Audience was updated by going to Audience Manager and checking the date below the column that says "Availability".

THE ULTIMATE FACEBOOK LEAD MACHINE

Chapter 19: Facebook Business Success Stories

Using innovative Facebook marketing strategies can transform your business, increasing your customer base, sales and income. One of the best ways to improve your Facebook business involves taking an active approach in building and maintaining your Facebook page.

This can include weekly or daily posts related to your product or service, as well as promotions and new offers. Remember, your fan base has already "liked" your page, therefore, you can leverage your fan base by providing them interesting content that they will share with their friends.

Many businesses have used Facebook to significantly increase their success. Below are some examples of Facebook success stories, how they succeeded and tips on how you can apply some of their concepts to your business.

The Peach Truck

Based in Nashville, Tennessee, The Peach Truck is a grocery store that tours extensively in the summer months selling peaches at summer events throughout the eastern and southern United States. Also, The Peach Truck offers gift boxes with peaches through its online presence that can be ordered online and delivered directly to the customer's address.

In order to introduce their products to new communities in the United States and increase their online sales for its

Georgia peach gift boxes, the company planned the Peach Truck Freestone Tour in 2015. To advertise the tour, CEO Stephen Rose and his team developed a series of link ads and boosted posts for Facebook.

To illustrate their mouth-watering peaches, the company used color saturated lifestyle photos of people eating and enjoying peaches in their link ads. Along with the graphics, they included price information and a link to the full tour schedule.

To spark interest and build a rapport with the audience, the ads targeted women over the age of 18 that lived within a 25 mile radius of all of the Peach Truck's tour stops. In addition, the targeted audience's interests included cooking, gardening, local produce, and that they shopped at Trader Joe's or Whole Foods.

The ads would run 24 hours a day on people's desktop and mobile news feeds one week before the Peach Truck's arrival to the tour stop, reaching the largest possible audience. For the Peach Truck's gift box service, the company developed a lookalike audience, which they based on an existing client email list.

The link ads were then developed providing the right focus for marketing the gift boxes. A Shop Now button would direct the customer to the Peach Truck's retail landing page where they could then place their order.

CEO Stephen Rose, commenting on the success of the tour said that:

"To see 300 people standing in line in a parking lot waiting for our peaches in a town we had never been to before was unbelievable. Facebook was the reason those people came out. They learned about us from this incredible platform, and we can't imagine a better way to interact with current and potential customers."

The Peach Truck's numbers are impressive. According to Facebook, as a result of the 2015 Freestone Tour, the company's growth in sales more than doubled on a year over year basis. In addition, over 50 percent of the company's tour clients were acquired through Facebook, with a 40 times return on their ad spending.

Sparkle in Pink

Based in Utah, Sparkle in Pink was founded in 2011 by mother and daughter Quynn and Diane Larsen. The company offers high fashion clothing for little girls at wholesale prices.

Sparkle in Pink was started by Quynn when she noticed how difficult it was to keep her daughter looking fashionable with the lack of choices and value that were then available. Diane and Quynn's principal marketing objective on Facebook is for customer acquisition and sales conversions, which they most effectively achieve using Facebook slideshow ads.

Having used Facebook, Sparkle in Pink ran several successful Facebook ad campaigns using formats such as carousel, which took customers directly to their product page. The carousel format worked great, but made certain products sell out too quickly. To make sales more even-paced, Quynn opted for slideshow ads.

From her past experience, Quynn was aware that the ads that performed best were the ones featuring new products, which were usually displayed on the homepage. She then developed slideshow ads for Facebook and Instagram, which would direct customers to Sparkle in Pink's homepage, where customers could check out new arrivals.

After trying various slideshow options, Quynn discovered the winning formula for their company: longer slideshows with a simple presentation and no sharp copy. The slideshow also includes a "Shop Now" button and targets four main audience segments based on clients' previous engagement with the Sparkle in Pink website and Facebook Page.

The company achieved a nine percent growth rate in monthly sales between November of 2015 and January of 2016, while only spending $1.00 to $3.00 per acquisition. This comes to a six times lower cost per acquisition with slideshow ads on Facebook than with any other social media channel.

Raising brand awareness through slideshows has proven to be the most efficient way of increasing conversions at the lowest possible cost for Sparkle in Pink. According to CEO Quynn Larsen:

> *"We used slideshow ads to send people to our homepage to see the new product arrivals. The*

return on ad spend has been incredible for us. We're really excited about slideshow because it's the best-performing format that we've found on Facebook and Instagram so far. We've now increased our budget to see how far we can go."

Lowe's Home Improvements

Providing home improvement products to more than 17 million customers a week, Lowe's is one of the largest retail chains of its kind. Based in Mooresville, North Carolina, Lowe's Companies, Inc. was founded in 1946 and is a Fortune 500 company, as well as a component of the S&P 100 and the S&P 500 indexes. The company's stock trades on the New York Stock Exchange under the ticker symbol "LOW".

With retail outlets in the United States, Mexico, Canada and Australia, Lowes stores stock approximately 40,000 products with more than 250,000 items offered online at their website and half a million products available through Special Order. Lowe's sells practically every homebuilding product to build a home from the foundation to the roof, and is the second largest hardware chain in the United States.

Lowe's Facebook goal was to raise brand awareness and encourage millennial and younger homeowners to improve their homes through affordable do-it-yourself projects. The company also wanted to present itself as a go-to partner and resource to new homeowners for renovations and repairs.

THE ULTIMATE FACEBOOK LEAD MACHINE

Partnering with New York based advertising giant BBDO as their ad creative, the company launched a 10-week Canvas campaign in the "Coordinated Style". Lowe's objective was to give its target audience of young new homeowners a complete designer experience, which it was able to achieve through Canvas. The ads were geared towards homeowners in the age range of 25 to 34 years old, which would often seem put off by what they assumed was the difficulty and expense associated with making improvements on their home.

The Canvas mobile ad format gives the viewer a complete brand experience, allowing them to immerse themselves and interact with the ad, giving the customer a way to make purchases without leaving Facebook. The ads depicted a simplified method of redesigning a living space, with attractive graphics of home interiors and text that prompted viewers to examine the "expert behind" the design by tapping on the ad and opening the full screen feature.

Once open, the full screen feature would allow the viewer to tour a variety of room designs, get information on specific details for the products integrated into each design, and to purchase the product instantly at the tap of their mobile device screen without leaving Facebook. The campaign was extremely successful, awakening interest in people to explore the special value provided by Lowes.

The Canvas campaign ran for ten weeks between November of 2015 and January of 2016, in which Lowe's obtained the following results: customers spent an average time of 28 seconds on Canvas, with the company making a return of 6.7 times on ad spend. According to Brad Walters,

THE ULTIMATE FACEBOOK LEAD MACHINE

Lowe's Director of Social Media & Content Strategy:

> *"Facebook's Canvas enabled us to tell a compelling home improvement story outside the confines of a typical News Feed ad. This allows customers to get a complete understanding of Lowe's coordinated style without ever leaving the platform. The experience provides a unique opportunity for the customer to explore the path of inspiration to conversion seamlessly."*

The above examples are just a small sample of how diverse types of businesses used different ad approaches to engage clients, increase sales and offer their products and services to new clients. One of the most valuable aspects of Facebook applied to advertising is the targeting of potential customers based on their Facebook Page, Likes and other metadata.

The Peach Truck example clearly illustrated how by awakening interest in their juicy product through attractive photo ads, which they ran continuously a week before their arrival to each town on the tour. The company was able to arrive to expectant crowds, waiting to buy their products and making the tour a huge success.

The company also benefitted by simultaneously promoting their gift boxes, and doubling their overall sales year to year after the tour. The amount of money the Peach Truck spent on Facebook was a fraction of what a radio or television campaign would have cost and probably considerably more effective.

Glossary of Facebook Related Term Definitions

Facebook users and web designers have developed their own jargon to communicate social media concepts, commercial arrangements and other pertinent information on the platform. In many cases, the terms that are used may seem initially familiar since they were originally used to describe traditional concepts.

Nevertheless, their relevance to social media and the context in which they are used often requires a more in-depth definition. The terms below have been compiled from Facebook and other sources to give the reader an understanding of the words as they apply to the Facebook platform and the subjects covered in this book.

About Section

An area of Facebook that contains basic information about your Facebook Page. Different basic information in the About section of the page will be displayed depending on the Page's category.

Ad

A term that describes the unit of what is being advertised, such as a Page, a website, a post, an app, an event or business; where the Ad is being advertised, for example, to the News Feed, a sidebar, desktop or mobile device; and the target audience, which includes their age, location, gender, lists and habits, as well as the method of bidding, such as CPM, CPC or Optimized CPM.

THE ULTIMATE FACEBOOK LEAD MACHINE

Account Settings

The area of Facebook where you can manage and edit all of your accounts' basic preferences, including name and email address, notification preferences and security features to name only a few.

Activity Log

The log is an aide to managing your Page's Timeline. The Activity Log is only available to people that help manage the page and displays a complete list of all of the posts and comments on your Page, including posts that have been hidden.

Admin Panel

An area of Facebook where Page administrators can edit pages, view insights, new page likes and comments.

App

Applications developed by third parties for Facebook that add additional features and functionality to the Facebook experience.

Audience Retention

A metric that gives details on video views. This metric tracks views continuously as a percentage of all views, which include videos of less than three seconds in length.

Badge

A personalized box that you create on Facebook to share a profile, a Page, photos or other information on other websites.

Boost Post

The Boost Post option gives the Post a higher rank in the News Feed. This gives the post a better chance to be viewed by a larger audience. Any post created on Facebook can be boosted, which includes photos, videos, status updates and offers to name a few. The amount charged by Facebook to boost a post varies depending on how many people you want reached.

Broad Category

Broad Category targeting is an advertising strategy that allows advertisers to target Facebook users that have a particular type of information or actions taken in their Timelines that have a common element with specific interests.

Campaign

The structure that holds your ads together. A way to organize similar ads together. Can hold many ads within it. This is where the overall ad budget (daily or lifetime) and start/end dates of promotion are determined.

Chat

A Facebook feature that provides users with an instant messaging service. The feature consists of a sidebar that allows users to conduct conversations with their Facebook friends free of charge. Facebook Chat supports one on one chat with an individual or chats with multiple friends using the Facebook Groups feature.

Check-ins

An action that announces a person's location to their Friends on Facebook. If the Page of the Friend checking in includes an address, it will appear on a list of possible locations to check when people are in close physical proximity. After the person has checked in, a story is created on their Friend's News Feed.

Click

This term is used quite often in different contexts on Facebook. The All Clicks metric counts the different types of clicks on your ad including links to other destinations, certain interactions with the ad container and links to expanded ad experiences. The All Clicks metric includes:

- Link Clicks, which refers to the number of clicks on ad links to particular destinations or experiences within Facebook and/or on other websites.
- Clicks to give post reactions, which include Likes and Loves.
- Clicks to expand media to full screen, which are those performed on imagery inclusions like photos or

videos
- Clicks to a profile picture or associated business page
- Clicks to take specific actions towards your campaign objective.
- Clicks to Comment on or Share a post.

Click Through Rate or CTR

The Click Through Rate is the number of clicks on an impression divided by the number of impressions per ad.

Connections

The possibility of targeting users based on connections to an app, event, Page or event within an advertiser's domain. For example Connections can be used to target users that have liked your Page, users that don't like your page or the friends of users that have liked your Page.

Conversion

A conversion is a customer completed action or transaction within a Facebook promoted business. This could consist of the purchasing of an item or adding a product to a cart on a business website.

Conversion Specs

A manual control for actions optimized when Optimized CPM is chosen. Ads of a particular action type such as Like, Page or Post Engagement for example, can be changed through Conversion Specs to perform a different action, such as photo view, link click or video play.

Conversion Tracking

A way for advertisers to optimize for and track certain specific offsite conversions, or Facebook tabs that are hosted externally. The conversions that can be tracked include registration, checkouts, add to cart, Key Page Views, Leads and other website conversions. Facebook can track these offsite conversions to help advertisers calculate their return on investment.

Consumptions

This metric reflects the number of clicks on your content which did not result in a story. Consumptions can be either Link Clicks, Video Plays, Photo Views or other clicks.

Comment

A Facebook feature that allows you to give feedback on a post.

Cost per Click or CPC

The Cost per Click represents the total cost divided by the number of clicks for each ad. When you create an ad, you can select this type of payment option manually in Facebook. Cost per Click bidding is an auction process that has the advertiser choose the maximum amount they would be willing to pay per click on their ad. Because the cost of the ad is determined by an auction process, the actual cost of the ad is determined by the competing bids.

Cost Per 1,000 Impressions or CPM

When you create an ad, you can select this type of payment option manually in Facebook. Cost per Click bidding is an auction process that has the advertiser choose the maximum amount they would be willing to pay per 1,000 times the ad was shown.

Count of Fans Online

This metric shows the number of your fans that are online per hour or by day to view content from any source.

Custom Audience

A Facebook feature that allows the advertiser to target specific customers. These customers can come from a Facebook User ID (UID) list, a Facebook App UID list, an email list or a phone number list for example.

Cover Photo

A large graphic, most often a photograph of the Facebook member at the top of a Facebook Page. The Cover Photo is public, so that anyone visiting your Page can see it. A photograph or graphic image that best represents your brand is highly recommended for your Cover Photo.

Daily Active Users

This metric is the number of people who have viewed or interacted with your Facebook Page on a specific day. It's categorized by the type of action they perform.*Daily Likes

The number of likes your Page has received on a particular day.

Daily Like Sources

The exact location that a user selected to give your page a Like.

Daily Page Activity

A metric that gives a breakdown on how people engaged with your Facebook Page on a specific day other than by Liking or commenting on your posts. The Daily Page Activity allows you to see when Fans post to your Page, upload videos or photos, mention your Page to Friends or write reviews.

Daily Story Feedback

A metric that gives a break down on how people responded to your stories through engagement via Likes and Comments. Feedback is also given by unsubscribing, which means that your stories will not appear in the unsubscriber's future News Feeds on a particular day.

Daily Unlikes

The number of Like removals your page received from fans on a particular day.

Domain Sponsored Story

The promotion of user shares from a domain in your control. Facebook automatically generates Sponsored

Stories based on shares from a domain once it is claimed by a Facebook user based on shares from your website.

Engagement

All actions performed by people on your Facebook Page. Engagement can consist of a share, a post Like, a click on a link, comment or image.

Engaged Fans

The number of fans that have clicked on any of the content on your Facebook Page, whether or not a story was generated.

Engaged Users

The number of unique users that have clicked on any of the content on your Facebook Page, whether or not a story was generated.

Engagement Rate

The number of unique users that have Liked, Shared or Commented on your post after being served an impression.

Event

A feature of Facebook that lets you organize events, respond to invitations, receive RSVPs and to monitor what your Friends are doing.

External Referrers

The amount of views generated on your Facebook Page that originated from website URLs that are not a part of Facebook.

Fan Impressions

This metric represents the number of times that the content on your Facebook Page was shown to fans in an ad, on your Timeline, Ticker and News Feed. Each unique fan can be shown multiple different impressions.

Fan Paid Impressions

The number of times that the content on your Facebook Page was shown to fans on your Timeline, News Feed or Ticker through an ad.

Fan Reach

A metric that counts the number of unique fans that were served at least one of your content impressions through and ad, Ticker, Timeline or News Feed.

Fan Paid Reach

The number of unique fans that were served at least one impression of content on your Facebook Page via the Timeline, Ticker, or News Feed through an ad.

Fans

In many places on Facebook, such as Page Insights, "fans"

refers to people that have Liked your Page.

Follow

An action taken on Facebook that allows you to keep track of people that you are interested in. By using follow, you can get items on your News Feed and updates that are of interest to you.

Friend

A Friend is a person that you connect with and share on Facebook. Facebook Friend requests can be sent and received to and from other Facebook members and require that both parties confirm the Friendship before becoming official. *Friending* is the action of sending a person a Friend request.

Friends of Fans

The unique individuals that are Friends with people who have Liked your Facebook Page. This metric represents the total potential reach of the content published on your Facebook Page.

Frequency Distribution

A metric that breaks down the number of unique users that were served with an impression of content from your Facebook Page by frequency. For example, from one to ten times, 11 to 20 times, or more than 21 times.

Groups

Dedicated spaces on Facebook for specific groups of people. Group members have the ability to share updates, documents, photos and can message within the Group. Groups can be public, limited to certain people such as co-workers for example or private.

Gender and Age

Two demographic metrics that detail the percentage of people that viewed any content on your Page by age and gender. The metric is based on information people have entered in their personal profiles.

Impressions

The impressions metric shows how many times a post from your Page is shown, whether the post is clicked on or not. Multiple impressions of the same post may be seen by the user, for example, someone might see a Page update in News Feed once, and then a second time if a friend of theirs shares it.

Insights

A metric that allows you to monitor the effectiveness of your Facebook post. As a Page administrator, you can see whether people are engaging in the content that you publish, with information such as Page likes, post shares and post reach.

THE ULTIMATE FACEBOOK LEAD MACHINE

Label

An action taken in Facebook's Power Editor to tag individual ads and campaigns in order to organize promotional material. The promotional material can be organized by Page, account, promotions, etc.

Lead Ad

A type of Facebook ad that is used by advertisers to collect business information such as price estimates, follow up calls and other data. The lead ad is also useful for collecting sign-ups for newsletters and other important information for your business.

Lead Generation

Lead generation is the building up of interest in a business's products or services. To do this, businesses often create campaigns that encourage consumers to fill out a form with their contact information.

Lookalike Audience

A feature that allows you to create an audience of users that are much like the users contained within a chosen Custom Audience. Facebook uses an offline customer list to analyze and generate a similar list for you that you can also choose the size of.

Like

A way to give positive feedback on a post or a page.

Clicking the "like" button on a post or a page lets you connect with people and products that might interest you or your business. When a Page is liked, the person liking that Page will begin seeing stories from that Page in their News Feed, the Page will appear on their profile, while that person will appear as a person that liked the Page.

Message

A private message between you and another user. It can be a "live" chat message if the user is currently online, or it can be sent as a message to their Facebook inbox. Live Chat is only available to individual users, and not to a business page.

Milestone

A type of Page post that allows you to highlight important items from your Page's Timeline. Milestones can be used to share events describing what you and /or your business are about.

Monthly Active Users

A metric that shows how many people have viewed or interacted with your Facebook Page over the last 30 days. Keeping track of this metric shows to what degree your Facebook Page's influence fluctuates on a monthly and seasonal basis.

Notifications

A feature that updates activity on Facebook. For example,

you can get a notification when someone accepts a Friend request, or if an update is made to a particular Group that you belong to.

News Feed

A constantly updated stream of stories located in the middle of your Facebook homepage. The News Feed updates stories, links, videos, photos and Likes from other Facebook members, Groups and Pages that you are connected to.

Notes

A feature that allows you to use rich-text format to publish messages, which gives you more flexibility than publishing by simple updates. Notes also lets you tag other Facebook members and add photos to your formatted text.

Negative Feedback

An action that tells Facebook that you do not wish to see certain content, or conversely, when other users tell Facebook that they do not want to see your content. Examples of negative feedback include: unlike Page, report as spam, hide all and hide post.

Offer

A way for certain businesses, organizations or brands to share discounts with their clients by posting a discounted deal on a Facebook Page. Once the offer is claimed by a customer, they receive an email that they can present at the Page's physical location to obtain the discount.

Optimized CPM

A Facebook default setting for most ad types that automatically shows your ad to people within your target group that are most likely to react with a desired action, such as a Page Like, Post Engagement etc.

Organic Reach

The number of Facebook users that were shown at least one impression of your content through the Ticker, News Feed or Timeline without paid advertising.

Organic Leads

Events that occur when someone sees a lead ad, then tags a friend of theirs in it, and their friend subsequently submits a lead.

Page

The way Facebook users connect with other users and share their stories. In addition to individual users, businesses, brands and organizations use Facebook Pages to reach their clientele and potential customers. Pages can be customized by posting stories, adding apps, hosting events etc. People that Like your Page get updates in their News Feeds.

Page Admin

The designated administrator of the Facebook Page. The

Page Admin is automatically designated upon the Page's creation, assigning the creator of the Page as the Page Admin. The Page Admin is the only person that can change the appearance and posts on the Page, and can assign roles to other people to assist in managing the Page.

Page Roles

Tasks assigned by the Page Admin to help manage Facebook Pages. Roles that can be assigned by the Page Admin include admin, advertiser, analyst, editor and moderator. To work on the Page, the person assigned to any of these roles must log into their personal account and work on the Page from there.

Page Views

The total number of times the Facebook Page was viewed during a specified time period.

Paid Reach

The number of unique Facebook users that were served with at least one impression of your content through the Ticker, News Feed or Timeline with an ad.

Pixel

A plugin that lets you measure how effective your advertising is by the actions taken by people on your website. Pixel data can help you build an advertising audience, unlock additional advertising tools, and ensure that your ad is being shown to the right people.

THE ULTIMATE FACEBOOK LEAD MACHINE

Placement

Where your Facebook ad will be displayed, which can be all of Facebook, Mobile or Desktop News Feeds, All Desktop or Right Hand Column only.

Post

An action taken by Facebook members to share content on their Facebook Page.

Post Attribution

Credit to the Facebook Page for comments, Likes and posts on the Page's timeline. Post Attribution lets the user attribute posts even if they are logged into Facebook as themselves and not the Page. A drop-down box allows the user to act as a Page or as themselves when creating a post or scrolling through the News Feed.

Post Clicks

The number of times people clicked on your content, whether or not the click resulted in a story.

Post Likes

The number of Likes on your Page posts that came from people viewing your ad.

Reach

The number of people that received impressions from a

Page post.

Search

A tool for finding people, Pages, Groups, apps, photos, videos and events on Facebook.

Social Plugins

Tools that other sites can use to give people active personalized social experiences. When interacting with social plugins, experiences off Facebook can be shared with Friends on Facebook.

Sponsored Story

An action that promotes a story, for example, Likes, comments, check-ins and shares, which are related to whatever is being promoted. Promoted items can be apps, events, posts, Pages or domains.

Story

A term used to describe the different ways that people can interact with your Facebook Page. These include:

- A Like on your Facebook Page
- Sharing, commenting or Liking a post on your Page
- Mention of your Page within other people's posts
- Tagging your Page in an uploaded graphic
- Answering a question that you asked on your Page
- A response to an event posted on your Page

- Checking in on your Page or a recommendation

Tabs

The sections included in your Page when it is created. Tabs keep your Page organized and allow people to see specific content such as photos, videos or events.

Tagging

An action that links a person, Page or location to an item that you have posted, such as a photo or status update. For example, a photo can be tagged to say who is in it or a post with a status update can say where you are or who you are with.

Ticker

A section on the right side of your homepage that updates your Friend's activities in real time.

Talking About This

A metric that shows the number of unique users that generated a story about your content.

Timeline

A collection of stories, photos and other experiences that illustrate your particular story. The Timeline acts as your Profile Page and contains all of your posts, videos, Friends List, interests and activities. The Timeline also includes any biographical information you choose to share, and lets your Friends leave messages. The Timeline is where you update your group of Friends with whatever you feel like sharing.

Total Reach

The number of unique users that were served with at least one impression from your content through and ad, the News Feed or your Timeline.

Total Impressions

The number of times that your content was displayed on an ad, your Timeline, Ticker or News Feed. A single unique user can be shown several impressions.

Upload

The action of adding content to your Page, Timeline or News Feed.

Unlikes

The number of unique individuals that have removed their Like from your Facebook Page during a specified time period.

Video Views

Total number of times that a video you have posted on your Page has been viewed for at least three seconds or more.

Index

THE ULTIMATE FACEBOOK LEAD MACHINE

THE ULTIMATE FACEBOOK LEAD MACHINE

www.ingramcontent.com/pod-product-compliance
Lightning Source LLC
Chambersburg PA
CBHW040931030426
42334CB00007B/107